WEBSITES

WEIRD WEBSITES

JESSICA ASHBY

JOHN BLAKE

In loving memory of Timothy Patrick Newman
21 December 1977 – 24 February 2007

Published by John Blake Publishing Ltd,
3, Bramber Court, 2 Bramber Road,
London W14 9PB, England

www.blake.co.uk

First published in paperback in 2007

ISBN 978 1 84454 423 3

British Library Cataloguing-in-Publication Data:

A catalogue record for this book is available from the British Library.

Design by www.envydesign.co.uk

Printed in the UK by CPI Bookmarque, Croydon, CR0 4TD

1 3 5 7 9 10 8 6 4 2

CONTENTS

INTRODUCTION

WELCOME TO THE wacky world of Internet weirdness at it finest. Throughout this book you'll witness a plethora of carefully handpicked sites for you to feast your eyes and ears on. (Those without sound, just your eyes.)

In today's fast-paced world of technology, the Internet is an integral part of our lives and is used on a daily basis by the majority of people worldwide either as part of their jobs or to communicate with loved ones in far-off lands. Some use it for educational research, while others might log on at the end of a long, hard, strenuous day as a form of recreation to wind down.

Whatever the reasons, the Internet has something for everyone and, if what you're looking for isn't there, you can simply create it. This is what makes the Internet unique and why this book has been written, since it not only depicts the accessibility of the Web in people's lives, but also reflects how diverse we are as human beings and gives us an insight into what makes people tick.

The Internet can be seen as the window to humanity's soul, getting a voyeuristic look into the thoughts and opinions of strangers from all walks of life, all over the world, and in some cases it teaches us a lot about ourselves. We are able to access information on just about anything, some we may want to see and some that is simply there to arouse our temptation and curiosity. We take the amount of information available to us for granted and it's hard to imagine how we managed without the Net.

What is weird to some may be the norm to others, depending on the context in which the information is displayed – meaning that pretty much any site could have qualified for this book. With millions of websites out there, I have managed to narrow it down to a choice few that will entertain, shock, inform, repulse and educate people in many different ways. Some sites you may find interesting and others not to your taste, but keep an open mind and a sense of humour if you wish to get through this book unscathed.

ANIMALS

WE ALL LOVE animals, some undoubtedly more than others, but with so many diverse creatures on the planet this chapter shows us what lengths people will go to in order to declare their love for their chosen animal. With people marrying their pets, adopting bats and buying replica dog poo as gifts for their loved ones, I have given you an insight into the strange world of the animal kingdom that is leaking its way across the Internet as we speak.

:: PET PSYCHICS

Ever wondered what's going through the mind of your cat? Or why your dog is so miserable? Has your bunny lost his bounce since witnessing the brutal murder of his brother by the neighbourhood fox? Well, I believe I've found the answer to your problems in one simple website. Browse through a bevy of psychic beauties all wanting to help you in your quest to communicate with your troubled pooch. And all this is done online without the need for them to even meet the animal – fascinating stuff. Of course, nothing comes for free, but I'm sure you'll agree at a reasonable £1 per minute it's worth every penny. A word of advice: keep them focused on the pet, otherwise it may turn into a very expensive online chat, unless that's what you were looking for all along!

http://www.psychicsdirectory.com

★ ★

:: AMAZING PREHISTORIC DOGS

Ever wanted a pet dinosaur? Well, these prehistoric dogs are the nearest you are likely to come to getting one. They are thought to be a distant relative of the well-known dinosaur *Thrinaxodon*, and there are four main breeds to choose from. With sightings as far afield as North Africa and London, there is sure to be one coming to a town near you. They are dying out fast and are hard to come by, but I figure a glow-in-the-dark Delta Skrimpy is well worth holding out for, don't you?

http://freespace.virgin.net/paul.charlton1/home.htm

★ ★

:: WHAT'S NEW, PUSSYCAT?

While we humans spend all our time on networking sites such as MySpace and Facebook, it's only fair that our precious pussies should get their fair share of Net exposure. Scroll through pages of cats finding out everything from their favourite food, to how many lives they have left. If you're feeling generous, you can leave them a piece of fish, or vote for them to be Cat of the Week. Our feline friends go all out: with items such as 'How *kool* is your cat?' and picture parties, you're sure to have a purrfect time on this site, which hits you with: 'Welcome To Catster, Where Every Cat Has A Webpage!' For its sister site, the doggie equivalent, try www.dogster.com.

http://www.catster.com
http://www.dogster.com

★ ★

:: LAB MONKEY

Welcome to the website of Edgar Frog. Now, before I continue, I must point out that Mr Frog is in fact a lab monkey, and not a frog, and he is trapped with a bunch of other animals in the Nevada Institute of Mental Health in Las Vegas, Nevada. He has an extreme dislike for humans due to the fact that he has been transformed into a cyborg monkey with his head on wheels. Can you blame him? There's loads to see and do on the lab monkey's site and you can even meet his equally intriguing creator. Be sure to check out Mr Frog's theories on 11 September – a must-see.

http://members.aol.com/EdgarFrog/index.html

★ ★

:: VAPOORIZE

Don't you just love it when you see fictional things in movies or on the television that make it on to their own website – especially when the topic in question is something imperative such as, let's say, dog-poo cleaner? Well, this website features the answer to every dog owner's prayers. Vapoorize – it's the only dog-poo cleaner that actually makes the poo vanish into thin air – really, it does! As featured in the movie *Envy*, the website shows the Vapoorize infomercial as well as listing testimonials from so-called 'happy customers'. Oh, and did I mention that the comedy actor Jack Black features throughout?

http://www.vapoorizer.com

★ ★

:: DOG JUDO

Brilliant website showcasing the talents of a cockney judo-obsessed dog and his ballsy sidekick, Rexley. Browse through the video archive where you will find short films of the duo in various comedic situations, based on the theme of judo of course. Watch him try his hand at dating, fire safety and avoiding bullets. A must-see site for everyone who loved BBC's *The Office*, Guy Ritchie's film *Lock, Stock and Two Smoking Barrels*, and anyone who is generally interested in a judo-obsessed dog with a black belt.

http://www.dogjudo.co.uk

★ ★

:: FROGS

A complete compilation of everything you could possibly want to know about frogs. Frogs in the news, weird frog facts, a frog art gallery, international frogs, frog speak, frog bread, a frog shopping guide, frog jokes, morphing frogs and a massive frog picture gallery – and not a word about Frenchmen.

http://allaboutfrogs.org

★ ★

:: DO YOU LOOK LIKE YOUR DOG?

This website invites you to send in your photos and be judged on the age-old question: do you look like your dog? Get the chance to take part in their annual competition, in which you and your pooch will feature in a book creatively entitled *Do You Look like Your Dog?*. Or get involved in workshop programmes, where you can learn about other dogs and their owners. You'd be barking mad to miss this one.

http://www.doyoulooklikeyourdog.com

★ ★

:: CUTE CORE

Whether you are a lover of animals or not, this website will have you turning all mushy as you browse through the adorable animal pictures. Nothing more than a library of people's pets, this simple yet effective site will have you glued to your screen for hours, browsing through pictures of these cute animals exploited for your pleasure. This site will turn the coldest of hearts into big fluffy marshmallows, and will make grown men coo like little babies; well, it's got to be worth a visit then.

http://www.cutecore.com

★ ★

:: FANCY A MONKEY IN YOUR MAILBOX?

Monkey Mondays is a website created by artist Rob Elliott. Quite simply, every Monday he sends out a monkey drawing to his subscribers, who eagerly await their Monday-morning fix of monkey madness. The website has been going strong for six years now, and, with no sign of the demand for monkeys in mailboxes easing up, it's no wonder Rob has branched out into merchandising Monkey Mondays on T-shirts and posters. And, on that note, I'm off to sign myself up for some Monkey Monday light relief.

http://www.monkeymondays.com

★ ★

:: BATS

Ever wanted to be the proud parent of a bat? Well, now you can. This site enables you to adopt your very own bat, or to recommend a responsible friend to do so. As the new parent, you will receive an official adoption certificate, a photograph of your chosen bat, an endearing letter from your new offspring and a super-duper BATTY ABOUT BATS bumper sticker. Browse the site for all you need to know on the subject of bats all around the globe to help you become a better parent to your nocturnal pet.

http://www.batcon.org

★ ★

∷ MIND THE DOG POO!

Having to avoid dogshit in the street is bad enough, but you would think in the privacy of your own home or workplace you would be free of the retched dung heap. But now, with the magic of technology, I am pleased to inform you that we are able to buy real-life replicas on the Net. To be used purely in the name of practical joking, of course! You can order online and choose from a range of different shapes, sizes and colours, complete with a heat-sealed bag and gift wrapping. You can even read up on the dog that allegedly laid the turd, making the whole experience that little bit more authentic. Maybe a virtual poop-a-scoop site wouldn't go amiss!

http://www.dogdoo.com

★ ★

:: CANINE VOYEURISM

Picture it. You've had a hard day at the office and the thought of curling up in front of the TV is a far-off dream when you're faced with the wall of traffic ahead of you. Pretty much nothing is going to distract you from your daily sulk except when a Ford Fiesta pulls up beside you with a cute doggy sitting in the passenger seat. Go on, crack a smile! This site is dedicated to those moments. Feast your eyes on pages of galleries featuring household canines in various automobiles. Cute, if not a tad creepy.

http://www.dogsincars.co.uk

★ ★

:: PRO-TEST

Founded in January 2006 by a 16-year-old student, *Pro-Test* aims to raise public awareness of the advantages of animal testing and create an environment where scientists can be proud of their findings. They're a very outspoken team of people who are made public through this site, and you can meet them and even get involved. My guess is that PETA (People for the Ethical Treatment of Animals) are not great fans.

http://www.pro-test.org.uk

★ ★

:: THE DOG'S BOLLOCKS

Cosmetic surgery for animals. That is what this site is all about. Neuticles are testicular implants for animals. Not only will they give your dog 'the snip', so to speak, but will replace the old nuts with prosthetic ones, all in the name of pet vanity. Now, when walking your dog through the park, you can have peace of mind that he will behave himself in public, all the while keeping his street cred in tact with his manly balls still on show. And this is not restricted to dogs: neuticles are available for felines, equines, bovines or any pet that has been neutered, and are available in three different models and a variety of sizes. Browse through this site for size charts and prices, which I might add start from $59 for a small implant to $719 for a large implant. However, I did notice they make a substantial discount when you buy the pair together, depending of course on how many your pet had to start with!

http://www.neuticles.com

★ ★

:: MY CAT HATES YOU!

This website has been bringing its visitors sour-faced cats since 2000. It's a website dedicated purely to evil-looking cats, so you won't see any nice kitties here.

Browse through the archives of these seriously fierce-looking felines getting up to all sorts of mischief, or, if you're feeling particularly brave, order the calendar or the book, where only the most pissed-off pussies make the grade.

http://www.mycathatesyou.com

★ ★

:: DESIGNER PETWEAR

An extremely cute site, which for some may have you reaching for your barf bag. (See Travel and Tourism for a choice of bags.) Pucci Petwear has all your pets covered in terms of splashing out on clothes, accessories and toys – everything from winter coats to dog tags. It's a one-stop shop for all your pet-pampering needs. With thoughtful items such as matching handbags for both you and your pet, and a Jimmy Choo Slipper for a dog toy, it really is a designer pet heaven. Move over, Paris Hilton, we're coming through!

http://www.puccipetwear.com

★ ★

:: CAVYLAND

This site is dedicated to the lovable household pet the guinea pig. I have never understood the fascination –

from what I gather, they are a mix of rabbit, hamster and rat and nothing to do with pigs at all! I was fortunate enough to be on holiday when it was my turn to look after the classroom pet and missed out on the whole guinea-pig-bonding experience. I'll hand over to the experts for a more accurate explanation of what they are and their qualities as species on this planet and let you form your own judgement on these furry friends.

http://www.cavyland.org.uk

★ ★

:: MONKEY PHONE CALL

This site is living proof of how easy it is for websites to encourage people to part with their money over the Internet. At $10 a time, you can order your very own monkey phone call. Surprise your friends, or even your boss, with a monkey message from the Monkey Phone Call team. You simply place your order online and within the next five days the lucky person of your choice should receive their monkey message – it's that simple. Maybe you know someone who needs cheering up and would really appreciate a message from a monkey to kick-start their week. Unfortunately, this service is available only to residents of the USA, so all of us non-Yanks will have to find other ways of amusing ourselves.

http://www.monkeyphonecall.com

★ ★

:: SCARY SQUIRREL WORLD

On arriving at the site, you may find the cheery hoedown-esque music a friendly if not pleasant introduction. And on entering the site you will find everything you ever wanted to know about, er, squirrels. You are invited to share your theories on where these amazing creatures originated, watch films and play games. There is a lot to be learned here, but always be wary of the squirrel: they are not as cute and innocent as they may seem as you will start to find out on this site.

http://www.scarysquirrel.org

★ ★

:: RANDOM CHICKEN

This site aims to celebrate just how random chickens can be. You are invited to send in pictures and browse through archives of chickens and celebrate in their randomness. Plenty of games and 'Why did the chicken cross the road?' jokes that will keep you poultry embracers occupied for hours. Now, for all you hardcore random chicken lovers, sign up for a randomchicken.net email address, and if that's not enough get yourself a funky-chicken T-shirt so you can *really* show your love for the randomness of the chicken.

http://www.randomchicken.com

★ ★

∷ MARRY YOUR PET

You and your furry friend can make it official by having the online wedding of your dreams. Or, for the more flamboyant couple, why not get the marryyourpet.com team to plan your special day, tailor-made to both your desires. Share your special moments with the world by announcing your love, and have pictures of your wedding day put up on the site for all to see. Online weddings start from a mere $10 and go up to $200 for a more lavish affair. And, if it all turns sour, this site can even provide you with a quickie divorce!

http://www.marryyourpet.com

★ ★

MYTHOLOGY AND THE PARANORMAL

COULD IT BE that we are constantly searching for something beyond this life and it's our curiosity that is leading us to believe that we can see and hear things when really they are nothing more than products of our vivid imaginations? I've always been a strong believer of mind over matter and think that, if you condition your brain long enough to believe something is true, in your mind it becomes so. But it is impossible to ignore the unexplained, and, after visiting some of these sites, you might question just what is really out there. Fascination with the paranormal dates back hundreds of years and will continue for hundreds of years to come – and, if these questions are ever answered, society will find some other abnormality to be the subject of speculation, because the unexplained is the fantasy that we all cling to. Without it, life would be simply one-dimensional and the world would seem to be a far more boring place in comparison with its enigmas.

:: THE INCIDENT

This eerie website came about when Danish-born Balder Olrik visited a second-hand bookstore in Berlin in 1997. He stumbled across a book entitled *The Incident*, which contained pictures of paranormal activity. Three days after he had returned home, the book was stolen from his flat and, with only the copies of the pictures left, Olrik created this site in the hope of finding someone who can tell him more about the whereabouts of the book or indeed its meaning. You are invited to view the pictures online and leave any comments you may have for Mr Olrik to get him closer to the truth.

http://netsummary.dk/incident/intro.html

★ ★

:: ADULT CHILDREN OF ALIEN ABDUCTEES

Have you always felt as if you didn't belong, or have you ever been told that you are strange and unusual? Maybe you hold powers that are beyond your control and are constantly looking for answers to questions about yourself and your life. If this sounds like you, then it's possible you could be the result of 'exoterran interbreeding'. It may be worth sitting your parents down and asking them if either of them has had any paranormal experiences that may have led to their giving birth to you. But do this only if you are certain, because you might get thrown in the loony bin for making such wild accusations.

http://www.wheretruthlies.com/AlienAbductees

★ ★

∷ ALONE

If ghost hunting and all that surrounds it gets your juices flowing, then this is the site for you. Start off by browsing through the library of eerie images and play a 'Where's Wally?'-type game that involves seeking out the ghosts in the images. It's up to you to decide whether or not they are really there or whether the images you are seeing are down to digital enhancement or are indeed staged. Now you're in the spirit of things, read through some frightening tales and visit old creepy insane asylums to get you really spooked. Last, visit the music room, where you can hear terrifying sounds that will send a chill down your spine. If after all this you still want more, might I suggest sleeping in a graveyard overnight or, better yet, a morgue?

http://home.comcast.net/~allalone

★ ★

:: THE BOY IN THE BOX

This website was created to help solve the ongoing mystery of the infamous Boy in the Box – America's unknown child. The story dates back to 25 February 1957, when a young boy was found dead in a box in Philadelphia, Pennsylvania. The identity of the boy is still unknown, as is the murderer and the cause and method of his tragic death. This site is a plea to anyone with information on this case to come forward, with the hope that providing viewers with vital statistics on the case may trigger memories or hearsay that someone may be aware of. View pictures of evidence and the discovery site as well as pictures of the mystery boy's body. The boy has been named 'Jonathan' by some, in the hope that he can one day be laid to rest in peace.

http://americasunknownchild.net

★ ★

:: DREAM INTERPRETATION

This is your online guide to everything you ever wanted to know about dreams. We all have them, some more pleasant than others, but what do they mean? Are they predictions or merely our subconscious working overtime? Get your dreams interpreted here and find out what's really on your mind. Find out about why we have dreams and how our mind works from the theories of famous psychologists, or read through the dream bank to see if yours match up to others'.

http://www.dreammoods.com

★ ★

:: BIGFOOT

This is the Website for all Bigfoot enthusiasts to come and get the latest information about the big hairy Sasquatch that has allegedly been spotted across parts of the USA and Canada. Browse through all of the Bigfoot sightings or submit your own if you have been fortunate enough to witness and capture the legend. And all you extreme Bigfoot fans can book yourselves on an expedition, but be quick, because they are fast selling out. For the more sceptical among you, of whom I'm sure there are plenty, read up on the physical evidence and the history of Bigfoot to gain a greater understanding into why the creature has become such a phenomenon.

http://www.bfro.net

★ ★

:: URI GELLER

This is the website of the spoon-bending, mind-controlling telepathic Uri Geller. He first graced the media world in the 1970s with his phenomenal ability to bend spoons and then went on to hone his skills with other wonders by fixing broken appliances such as watches, by reading minds and by moving things with the power of thought (telekinesis). Read what the experts have to say about this eccentric man and their opinions on whether his skills are down to a paranormal gift or simply a form of magic, and find out if you are one of the rare people who are drawn to occurrences '11:11'!

http://www.uri-geller.com

★ ★

:: FORK YOU

Ever since Uri Geller came on the scene in the 1970s, bending of kitchen cutlery has become a household trick around the dinner tables of families worldwide. The people at Fork You don't see what they do as being paranormal. They consider their art form to be incredibly normal now they know how to do it. Their reason for bending forks and not spoons is that they see the pronged member of the place setting as being far more interesting, having extra bending possibilities, so you might want to consider that when choosing your cutlery to bend. Use their step-by-step online guide to start bending the forks in your kitchen, but make sure you have the permission of the people who eat with them first.

http://fork-you.com

★ ★

⦂ GHOST RESEARCHERS

This group of people eat, sleep and drink ghost life. Since 1977, this team of ghost researchers from the USA have been hunting down entities from the spirit world in order to gain a greater understanding of the 'other side'. To them, it's more than just a hobby: they carry out lectures on the topic as well as write books and make regular TV and radio appearances to talk about their skills. You too can become a member by taking part in their qualifying interview and paying a submission fee – only for hardcore ghost hunters, not for the curious.

http://ghostresearch.org

★ ★

⦂⦂ HAUNTED BRITAIN AND IRELAND

Planning a weekend away, but don't fancy travelling too far? Or maybe you're looking to stay somewhere that's a little bit different from your average hotel break. This website specialises in trips away that are like none you've ever experienced before. Book yourself a haunted break in Britain or Ireland and expect the unexpected for a truly unique experience. Stay in some of the country's oldest hotels and castles, renowned for their historic structure as well as their stories and spirits. So, if you are looking for a unique experience in beautiful historic surroundings and enjoy getting the crap scared out of you, this should be right up your street!

http://www.afallon.com

★ ★

:: CHANGE YOUR ASTROLOGICAL SIGN

This site is for all who believe they have been incorrectly assigned their zodiac sign. The Institute of Celestial Sciences believe they have broken the astrocelestial time barrier and are able to assign you a more fitting zodiac sign that will enable you to fulfil your potential in life. With no harmful side effects and no cost to this procedure, you have nothing to lose and everything to gain by changing your sign. All you need to do is fill out the online form and wait for the transformation to take place. Most people say they notice a change as soon as they press 'submit', so what are you waiting for? It could be your destiny.

http://www.jackrudy.com/ics/change.htm

★ ★

:: INTERSPECIES TELEPATHIC COMMUNICATION

This website came about when somebody injured their ankle and was healed as a result of receiving a telepathic message from their cat. More common occurrences happen with people suffering head injuries, but recent studies show that this type of communication happens on a daily basis around the world with people who are able to tune into other species and their thoughts. Join the hundreds of people across the world who have encountered telepathic communication between species by taking the time to listen out for messages from unexpected life forms. Well, if parrots can do it, there's hope for the others yet.

http://www.cyberark.com/animal/telepath.htm

★ ★

:: MAGICK WHISPERS

This is the website of a solitary witch and paganist who wishes to spread her lifelong study of her craft to those searching for a deeper understanding of witchcraft. Within this magical site are explanations on paganism, neo-pagan, witchcraft, Wicca, solitary magic, customs and the differences between witchcraft and Wicca. Learn the many crafts for becoming a witch and all that comes with the title, or even adopt a witch to gain greater insight into the craft.

http://www.magick-whispers.com

★ ★

:: MYSTERY MAG

Mystery Mag is an online magazine that provides daily reports on all the paranormal goings-on from around the world and beyond to give a greater insight into the unknown. Read articles on UFO sightings, ghost hunts and unsolved mysteries, leading you to make up your own mind about whether these encounters are really fact or fiction.

http://www.mysterymag.com/whatsnew/index.php

★ ★

:: MYSTIC BALL

Whether you believe in mind reading or not, this website will bamboozle you into thinking that it is possible. Simply follow the steps that the old wizard advises and be amazed at the results of the mystic ball. Once you have figured out how it works – and I'll be honest, it's not hard – send it to all of your unsuspecting gullible friends who wouldn't question its authenticity. A fun site up until the point that you realise it's a trick, which for all who are reading this starts from now.

http://www.mysticalball.com

★ ★

:: SETI

Making contact with extraterrestrials can be challenging at the best of times, but the team at the Search for Extraterrestrial Intelligence (SETI) have come up with a way of making the process more accessible to the masses, resulting in more communication with alien life forms. SETI is an organisation that aims to communicate with aliens and the likes by using the Internet to search for these types of intelligence. Download the software to start your research into the unknown and report back to base with your findings.

http://setiathome.berkeley.edu

★ ★

:: HAUNTED HOLLYWOOD

Hollywood is best known for its glitz and glamour, home to the stars and a place for fame-hungry wannabes. With its larger-than-life existence, people are drawn to it as though to a magnet and all want to be a part of its showbiz buzz. But underneath the costume and makeup of this entertainment capital is another side that often goes unnoticed: that of crime and corruption. Behind every theatre, home and street there is a horror story that has been overshadowed and swept under the red carpet by its shimmering camouflage. This website aims to extract the truth about Tinseltown and clean out its dirty closets by exploring a side of Hollywood that its citizens would rather forget existed.

http://www.prairieghosts.com/hollywood.html

★ ★

:: VERY SUPERSTITIOUS

Are you one of those people who won't walk under ladders or over three drains or break a mirror for fear that they'll be cursed with bad luck for ever more? If this is you, then read on, since this next website will give you the oldest superstitions around. But fear not: there are plenty of good-luck superstitions here too, so being paranoid can suddenly become fun for you. If you have managed to skip the OCD gene, you will probably find this site interesting to say the least. Not only did someone actually think up these superstitions, but some poor bastards actually believe in them. Not only did someone actually think up these superstitions, but some poor bastards actually believe in them. Sorry – I had to write that twice for fear that something bad might happen!

http://www.oldsuperstitions.com

★ ★

∷ HAUNTED EUROPE

Are you planning a romantic trip away and looking for something to spice it up a bit? Haunted Europe give advice on many haunted locations and accommodation throughout Europe that will ensure you and your partner will sleep close at night. They will put you in touch with holiday companies that will tailor-make you the perfect haunted trip, ensuring top quality all the way. Should you wish to pay good money to be scared out of your wits, I strongly recommend these guys.

http://www.afallon.com/international.htm

★ ★

∷ PARANOIA

Paranoia: The Conspiracy & Paranormal Reader is a magazine that goes to print three times a year. This is its website. With a strong team of authors and visionaries in the conspiracy, occult and paranormal genres, *Paranoia* aims to sift through the evidence of crime cases, terrorist attacks and government conspiracies and presents the other side of the story that is often kept out of the public arena. Take the online survey to help the magazine know more about its readers and the thoughts going through the minds of society, and find out the shocking truths of how corrupt your mind has become as a result of the world you live in.

http://www.paranoiamagazine.com

★ ★

:: STOP ALIEN ABDUCTION

Do you suffer from sleepless nights for fear that you will be visited by another species in your sleep? Or maybe you are fed up of being on the receiving end of telepathic communication between you and our extraterrestrial neighbours and want to break free from always being their guinea pig. This website is home to the thought-screen helmet, which promises to stop aliens communicating with humans and controlling their minds. Read the online steps to creating your own thought-screen helmet to prevent any more interferences with your brain, and start a new fashion trend in the process.

http://www.stopabductions.com

★ ★

:: STRANGE MAG

This website brings you up-to-the-minute news on all the strange and paranormal goings-on around the world. They cover all aspects of the weird and unusual, including anomalies, time travel, urban legends, hoaxes, supernatural, monsters, synchronicity, ESP, parapsychology and many other oddities that grace this world and beyond. Magazines like this aim to educate and inform people who are searching for a greater understanding of the world around them by taking their readers to another level of thought. Expect the unexpected with every issue as it is their mission to hunt out weirder material every time.

http://www.strangemag.com

★ ★

:: THE SCEPTIC'S DICTIONARY

This online word list may look like a normal dictionary, but it comes with a difference. Included in the list are words and phrases that are seen by some as nothing more than hocus-pocus and shouldn't be taken seriously. Many items included in the dictionary are part of everyday life, ranging from things people believe in to jobs they carry out. Read up on the true meanings of the words and phrases to gain a greater understanding, after which you may pass judgement as you see fit. And you can read the dictionary in a variety of different languages, including French, Hungarian and Japanese. So I guess that, if a mass of people consider these so-called strange beliefs to be the norm, they have every right to be used in a daily manner – hence the reason for this list.

http://skepdic.com

★ ★

∷ THE AMITYVILLE MURDERS

The story of the Amityville murders has been a high-profile mystery for over three decades now and its renowned media coverage is what has kept this enigma alive and will do so for many more years to come. The story arose in 1974, when police discovered six members of the DeFeo family dead at 112 Ocean Avenue in Amityville, New York. Since then, the story has been the topic of many different theories in the form of murder, the paranormal and even a sick media-infused hoax due to the Lutz family purchasing the property in 1975 and then fleeing very soon after as a result of what they claimed was an unnatural evil presence in the house. Within this site, you can read up on the full story and its associates to gain a greater insight into one of the biggest urban legends to date and make your own mind up as to whether the legend is indeed just that, or whether there is the possibility of a dark force greater than we could ever expect.

http://www.amityvillemurders.com

★ ★

:: THE FEDERAL VAMPIRE AND ZOMBIE AGENCY

This satirical website is the home of the Federal Vampire and Zombie Agency (FVZA), which claims to have been fighting to protect the world against such entities since its inception in 1868, stating that vampires arrived in the USA with some of the first European settlers. The site pays tribute to all who lost their lives while working for the FVZA in protecting their country from vampires and the like. The agency also seeks to raise awareness of current research that could potentially bring back an epidemic of the blood-sucking creatures worse than ever before. But fear not: the weapons-advice page should be of use in case you happen to stumble across an obsessive neck-loving partner in the near future.

http://www.fvza.org

★ ★

:: THE LEGEND OF NESSIE

Are you one of the few fortunate people to have caught a glimpse at the elusive legend that is the Loch Ness Monster? If so, you may find this site an interesting reference to your experience. Those who are still fascinated by the illusion of the creature but haven't been as lucky in their quest to get a peek can view this site as their eyes and ears into a world where the legend lives and breathes, which will hopefully help them fulfil their dream of viewing Nessie in all her glory.

http://www.nessie.co.uk

★ ★

:: THE PAGE THAT DRIPPED BLOOD

If you have a penchant for blood, this is the site for you. Created by horror enthusiast Patrick Olsen, this website brings you everything you ever wanted to know about the red stuff brought to you in a rather amateur way, giving it that edgy feel. This site gives an insight into a dark world of vampires and the macabre, depicting blood in films, places and ceremonies of love and death. Not for the faint-hearted or for those with a morbid fear of prosthetics, but a must-see sight for all fantasists and wannabe vampires who are too afraid to draw first blood.

http://www.drippingblood.com

★ ★

:: THE SALEM WITCH

This website takes you back to 1692, when the town of Salem, Massachusetts, and the then Salem Village were a paranoid breeding ground for witch hunters and protesters against devil worship. The paranoia was brought on by a concoction of many factors such as smallpox, conflict among neighbouring towns and the threat of attack on the area's people, making the people of Salem awash with fear and suspicion. The Salem Witch Museum was set up to document all the 17th-century goings-on that led to the deaths of 24 victims, all supposedly associated with witchcraft.

http://www.salemwitchmuseum.com

★ ★

:: THE HOUSE

This is an interactive website where you are invited to visit the deserted house of a family who all allegedly committed suicide in 1970. Take a tour around this haunted house and brave all the spooky goings-on. To get the full experience, you are advised to enter with the sound on to listen out for any clues as to what might have really happened to this family. Plenty of surprises and heart-pounding moments will keep you on the edge of your seat right up to when you leave.

See if you can brave it all the way through to find out the truth about the story of this sinister house and all the horror that happened behind closed doors.

http://fizzlebot.com/sinthai/thehouse.htm

★ ★

:: URBAN LEGENDS

This is the ultimate online explanation for all the urban legends that you have been carrying around with you since your childhood. They will all be put to rest once you've finished with this site with either confirmation that they do exist or denial, showing that you've been a gullible moron for most of your life and it's now time to consign these superstitions to the past. It is thoughtfully broken down into categories of genres and you can easily look up your myth of choice and find out about its authenticity. Plenty of shock value here with visual aids to support the statements – a site well worth spending some time on.

http://www.snopes.com

★ ★

ENTERTAINMENT AND GAMES

EVERYONE NEEDS SOME light entertainment from time to time and the Internet has fast become a virtual playground for jokes, games and other weird things for us to ogle at and use as either a distraction from life or as a good time filler for boring days. This chapter lists some top websites to spice up your lunch hour, or just pass the time if you are struggling to fill up your day with activity. But be warned: this chapter should not be looked at if you have important things to get on with, because the content is highly distracting and will almost definitely prevent you from continuing with any important duties you need to get done. If, however, you specialise in doing nothing all day, then this chapter will give you a reason to get up from the seat in front of the box and move to the seat in front of the PC, unless of course you have a wireless laptop, in which case you don't even have to move!

:: LIES

Fed up with the truth? If you think telling lies is fun, then this site is for you. The creators of the site have trawled the World Wide Web to compile a massive database of more than four thousand lies, on every topic from aardvarks to zymurgy. There's a Lie of the Day, Lies of the Week, Celebrity Liars and Guest Liars, and you can have a new lie – such as, 'The first 8,000 copies of Marvin Gaye's 1973 album, *Let's Get It On*, were made out of solid oak' – emailed to you every day. Be sure to use this site as only light relief from your monotonous life and not to let it rub off on your daily behaviour. Remember the tale of the boy who cried wolf, or maybe the little wooden boy would be a better reminder.

http://www.daveweboflies.com

★ ★

:: SILLY WALKS

Brought to you by *Monty Python*'s personal best is a website that enables you to create your very own unique silly walk in the style of your favourite character. Choose from four different characters and backgrounds to help you set the scene for your silly walk. For the less computer-literate, there is an online tutorial to talk you through the steps to creating your walk, but, to be honest, half the fun is working it out for yourself. Once finished, you can send it to a friend and invite them to create their own. Now all that's left for you to do is test it out on the streets. Good luck!

http://www.sillywalksgenerator.com

★ ★

:: PERPETUAL BUBBLE WRAP

Are you one of those people who can't resist ordering items online in the hope that they will arrive engulfed in bubble wrap to relieve tensions and annoy those around you by popping the plastic bubbles? Well, this site is one of the Internet's best-kept secrets and, if you haven't visited it yet, you'll be grateful for the introduction. Welcome to virtual bubble wrap, the site that provides you with sheets of the stuff so you'll never run out of bubbles to pop. Simply roll your mouse over the bubbles to see and hear that fulfilling pop that for so many of us is as satisfying as sneezing. Choose among sizes of bubbles; choose 'manic mode' (you don't even have to click your mouse!); even try to beat your score on how fast you can pop it all. Seriously addictive stuff – you have been warned.

http://www.virtual-bubblewrap.com

★ ★

:: ULTIMATE TAXI

Fancy a taxi ride with a difference? Driver and tour guide Jon Barnes has been taking passengers on the ultimate taxi-cab experience since 1984 in his vintage yellow taxi. Not only does it attract attention visually, but the second you step inside the doors you are hurled into a party atmosphere with music, lights and sound equipment. For those who aren't able to travel to Aspen, Colorado, Barnes has linked himself up to the Internet so you can share the experience from the comfort of your own computer. The Ultimate Taxi has fast become a media frenzy and, with stars like Clint Eastwood and Kevin Costner jumping in, rides in this cab are not cheap, but hey – you get what you pay for, I guess.

http://www.ultimatetaxi.com

★ ★

:: ANT CITY

This Channel 4 game site is host to one of the most satisfyingly macabre Internet games I have come across in a while. The concept is to kill and destroy as many people and objects as possible from an eagle-eye position with the use of a magnifying glass, burning them to a crisp. With great sound effects to match, there are no points to be won here, meaning there are no set levels of play, and, from what I can determine, the game is over only once you have managed to blow up the large petrol lorry, leaving an enormous crater in the ground. Take out your anger on the human race in this virtual world of unsuspecting citizens – should be right up most people's street.

http://www.channel4.com/entertainment/games/gameson4/ant_city.html

★ ★

:: TWENTY QUESTIONS

The classic game of Twenty Questions is brought to you in no fewer than twenty different languages. And the online game is just as much fun as playing the original with the family on Christmas Day. For those who have never played the game before, and shame on you if you haven't, the rules are quite straightforward. All you have to do is to think of a subject – animal, vegetable or mineral – and the computer will have twenty attempts at asking you questions that require a yes or no answer to determine what you are thinking. Get it? There are other pages to this site that specialise in genres such as music, TV, movies and even a kiddies' section for an easier option. To be played *only* during lunch breaks

so you can amuse yourself within a time frame –
otherwise you'll never leave this site.

http://www.2oq.net

* *

:: STARE DOWN SALLY

This is adapted from the childhood school game we all
used to find ourselves playing in those seemingly
endless maths lessons. The object is to outstare a
computer-generated image named Sally. Sounds
easy? Wait until you see Sally. She is an emotionless
character with piercing green eyes and a sweet but
extremely sinister face. Play a warm-up game to get
you in the swing of things before playing for real,
which could go on for a while. In all honesty, you will
almost always lose. I have yet to beat her and, believe
me, I've been staring hard at her. This is one of those
websites where you find yourself hiding behind your
hands for fear of what the sick site makers might
throw at you. Call me what you will, but that Sally is
one creepy lady who isn't going to be blinking any
time soon.

http://www.stairwell.com/stare

* *

:: FANCY A SINGSONG?

This site features an already published, lyrically and visually animated ode to the London Underground. We have all had our fair share of bad experiences on the Tube: delays, closures, strikes, hygiene issues, Oyster Card malfunctions, overcrowded platforms and carriages – the list goes on and on. No wonder London's commuters are miserable all the time: they are harbouring pent-up anger that they need to release. But, as soon as they make their way up to street level, they would rather forget about their nasty experiences and carry on with their day. Well, the guys who started this site have obviously been messed around by the Tube one time too many and have decided to focus their anger into this surprisingly catchy little number, which sums up the majority of commuters issues with London Transport. Plenty of profanities flying around in this harmonious outcry, and rightly so – this should be London's anthem. Brilliant!

http://www.backingblair.co.uk/london_underground

★ ★

:: 99 ROOMS

This website is a virtual maze by a creative team of artists, animators, graphic designers and sound technicians. Work your way through the 99 rooms by finding something within each destination that will lead you on to the next. Once you're deep inside, there's no turning back, and you'll find yourself alone and lost in a derelict warehouse full of eerie goings-on that will keep you in suspense right to the end. So what are you waiting for? Turn up your speakers and enter the creepy world of 99 Rooms for an unusual but worthwhile experience.

http://www.99rooms.com

★ ★

:: ADOPT A DEMON

You know you're just setting yourself up for trouble with this one. As if being a parent to a normal child weren't enough, these guys expect you to give up all your free time to care for a demon. There is a shop window of orphans on this site for you to choose from and invite into your own home/website, but adoption, as you may know, is not a straightforward process and not just anyone can become a guardian. Take the online steps to becoming the parent of a demon and finally, once you're accepted, make it official by registering your new offspring online. I myself am the proud parent of Demon 6, affectionately known to his friends and family as Puke – he's a right little devil.

http://adoptademon.50webs.com

★ ★

:: BIG HOAXES

Here lie all of those annoying emails that get sent to your inbox on a daily basis from your gullible friends and contacts. Every hoax under the sun can be found here. Most you will have probably seen already, but some may be new to you and you may be surprised to find out that they are in fact lies. There is also a section of true stories, and so some emails that may have sounded like hoaxes may be true. My suggestion to you is to send all these paranoid gossipmongers the link to this site and watch all your junk email disappear. I'm still not convinced that KFC is real chicken, but then I must have fallen for one of these hoaxes too.

http://www.bighoaxes.com

★ ★

:: BLACK HOLE OF THE WEB

Why is it that, when we are told not to do something, it makes us want to do it even more? You are advised on the home page of this site *not* to enter the black hole, but I guess if I ignored this warning it wouldn't have been included in this book, so I carried on regardless. Seriously nothing to see here except being plummeted further and further into the darkness that is the black hole. Once inside, you will realise that listening to the advice of people more experienced than you almost always pays off and saves you from feeling like a complete moron. Good luck finding your way out.

http://www.ravenna.com/blackhole.html

★ ★

:: FLASH MOUNTAIN

Warning! This site contains nudity on a hilarious level. If you don't have a sense of humour or have an adverse disliking to mammary glands, then turn back now. A website full of wardrobe malfunctions that will put Janet Jackson's 2004 Super Bowl appearance to shame. Really, this site is just another excuse to add to the endless stream of websites containing nude women. But the highlights for me, which amused me greatly, are the bevy of flashers on Disneyland's Splash Mountain ride. You can even submit your very own nude roller-coaster pictures to add to the collection.

http://www.flashmountain.com

★ ★

:: DRIBBLE GLASS

This website holds a collection of all the wackiest jokes, gifts and gags on the Net. There is plenty to see and do here with links to equally entertaining sites. Take a look at the billboards page, where advertisements that we'd all really like to see on our way to work are displayed. This site will also help you improve your memory by using visual aids to ensure that those facts will well and truly stick. Read up on all the current strange news from around the world, or, if you have time, stay for a while and have an interview with God.

http://dribbleglass.com

★ ★

:: WORLD'S SMALLEST WEBSITE

I thought I'd seen just about everything weird in the way of websites until I stumbled across this little gem. It's the world's smallest website, measuring just half a centimetre square, and the beauty of this site is that it is fully operational. You can actually navigate around this tiny little box, and its content includes 16 nostalgic games such as Pac Man and Ping-Pong, all to be played within its minuscule space. Great fun and very challenging, although on leaving the site you can still see tiny dots when you close your eyes and may suffer from a dull headache.

http://guimp.com

★ ★

:: HUMAN FOR SALE

It's something that people in modern-day society would never really think of, but, if you had to put a price on yourself, how much would it be? Are you the sort of person who thinks very highly of him/herself – healthy, good-looking, career-minded and law-abiding? Or do you readily admit that you are a greedy bastard who is unkempt and an outlaw? Well, this site will reveal all in a no-holds-barred test to see how much you are really worth. Can you face the fact that you may not be as worthwhile as you thought? Or have you been selling yourself short all these years only to find out that you are more valuable than you had ever imagined? Go on, have a go – you might surprise yourself.

http://www.humanforsale.com

★ ★

:: BORED?

This old faithful has been providing web users with endless hours of fun for years. One of the original distraction-from-life sites, it has more pointless but pleasurable activity than a cat has chasing its own tail. A great lunch-break site, or for those who have lots of boring but important jobs to get done and are itching for some form of distraction, this one comes highly recommended. Hours of futile fun to be had by all with quizzes, games, jokes and other great links to equally moronic sites that will have your day over in no time at all.

http://www.bored.com

★ ★

:: IS IT NORMAL?

This website allows you to find out how your life experiences compare with those of the rest of the world. Based on a poll, it allows you to post up on the site something that may have happened to you or something you are feeling, and others will vote to tell you if they think it is normal or not. Browse through other people's experiences and compare yourself with them, leaving your judgement on their unusual shenanigans. Choose among categories for a more detailed search and leave your comments or advice for people who are really clueless as to what to do in their situation.

http://isitnormal.com

★ ★

:: JERK YOUR OWN ADVENTURE

Here's one for the guys, but, girls, you're welcome to join in if you wish. The idea behind this site is to get through all the obstacles that keep getting in your way for you to be able to relieve yourself at the end of the mission. It's all about making the correct choices in finding the quickest route to your virtual bedroom, where you can carry out your act of self-fulfilment. Getting there isn't easy, though, and there are many wrong turns and dead-ends. However, fear not: there is a way through it, but don't expect anything wonderful at the end. Once there, you're on your own!

http://www.jerking.com

★ ★

∷ KARMA MACHINE

Are you one of those people who let their work dictate their lives and never have time for those closest to them? Maybe it's time you took a break from it all to do a good deed that, in return, may come back to you in one form or another. This website is the home of the karma machine, which allows you to send out positive messages to your nearest and dearest to let them know you are thinking of them. It's very simple to use: just type in your message and choose a picture to accompany it. Then wait for their response, or just feel all warm inside as you reflect on your good deed.

http://www.karmamachine.com

★ ★

:: DON'T CLICK HERE!

This is one of the best time-wasting sites around, where you are fully aware of the fact that the website is pointless but you can't help but continue to navigate. Its creators claim that there is nothing to see on the site and by following the links you are wasting your time. But I was quite amused by the amount of effort put into a site that supposedly contained nothing. The key is to ignore all instructions and do the exact opposite of what you're told. It's a battle of wills between man and machine, so be strong, people, and don't let the side down!

http://www.hat.net/abs/noclick/index.html

★ ★

:: MAKE YOUR OWN SNOWFLAKE

Feeling creative but have absolutely no artistic ability? Visit this site, where you are able to make your own snowflake using paper provided and a pair of virtual scissors. Once it's finished, you can display your festive creation in the online gallery for all to admire. I've always found it very therapeutic cutting things up into small pieces, and with this snowflake generator you can start all over again with a fresh sheet should you get a bit scissor-happy. A website so easy a child could use it. Actually, it probably *is* for kids. But who cares? There's a big kid in all of us, so rekindle your youth and get cutting.

http://snowflakes.lookandfeel.com

★ ★

:: SPOT THE SERIAL KILLER

What this website is cruelly, but observantly, pointing out is the visual similarities between serial killers and programme-language inventors. You will be faced with ten different pictures of sinister-looking guys with accompanying sound effects, and the object is to guess whether they prefer to hack into your computer or into your body. I scored a shameful four out of ten, meaning I'd better be more wary of that creepy IT guy at work. Come to think of it, one of those men did look kind of familiar.

http://www.malevole.com/mv/misc/killerquiz

★ ★

:: NOBODY HERE

You'll never get yourself out of this website, unless of course you find the secret key. This site, which is supported by the Netherlands Foundation for Fine Arts, Design and Architecture, is developed by Jogchem Niemandsverdriet, who leads us through a virtual maze of thoughts and observations. It's designed to get you well and truly lost within cyberspace, and you will find yourself with multiple links taking you to further pages with even more links. Don't try to work out how you got there. Just keep picking out different links and you may just find something of interest. But, before you start clicking on links, here's a heads-up for you: choose your language first of all or the whole experience will be lost.

http://www.nobodyhere.com

★ ★

:: NUDGER LOADER

Has someone you know been bugging you lately and you want to do something to get back at them? This nudger loader is designed for such jobs. Go through each of the vocal buttons to piece together the most offensive sentence you can muster, and then send it to Mr or Mrs Annoying's inbox. The trick is to do this when you know your victim will be at work to get them into even more trouble with the boss as their computer starts screaming out profanities. Now all you have to work out is which of your contacts to send it to. Well, that shouldn't be too hard!

http://www.godosomething.co.uk/startsomething/nudger_loader.htm

★ ★

:: THE WONTON WAY

This is the ultimate website dedicated to all things stupid. First created to rebel against the seriousness of the Internet, the site has grown in content to house some of the WWW's most ridiculous things. Watch a multitude of videos ranging from scientific experiments to silly speeches with no purpose other than to entertain the masses, providing a little light relief from their ordinarily sensible day.

http://www.wontonway.com

★ ★

:: RUDE MOUNTAIN

A spoof on the Internet greeting-card site Blue Mountain, this gives you the ultimate rude, crude and inappropriate cards on the Net. Show someone you love how much thought you have put in to getting them the perfect card that you know they will appreciate. Although not really the type of website you'd pick out your granny's birthday card on, it's bloody good for your mate Dave!

http://www.rudemountain.com/greeting/index.cfm

★ ★

:: SMALLTIME GAMES

This website has some seriously addictive games and activities that you'll be there all day long playing with, and then forward on for your friends to have a go. My two personal favourites are a game called Guess the Dictator/Sitcom character, which invites you to think up a character and through a succession of questions it will guess the very person you're thinking of; and The Anonymous Message Server, where on entering the site, there is an anonymous message waiting for you from the previous person and then it is your turn to leave a message for the next person. Get it? And there are many other places to visit on this site that will aid in making your day simply fly by.

http://www.smalltime.com/games.html

★ ★

:: SEEKING REVENGE?

We have all been in a position at one point in our lives where we feel we have been wronged by someone, be they a close friend or family member, or just one of those annoying people who most of us have the misfortune of dealing with on a daily basis, either through work or just by popping down the road to the shops. Now, for some, it's easy to turn the other cheek and rise above the situation, but for others, who are fed up with being a doormat and are ready to take some action and seek revenge, this website will more than whet your appetite for sweet retribution. Read through pages of stories, tips and hints from experienced revenge seekers to help you plot your way back to the top.

http://www.ekran.no/html/revenge

★ ★

:: THE COMEDY CORNER

Is the working day dragging? Are you craving some light entertainment to perk you back up to your usual jovial self? Comedy Corner provides a range of jokes, stories and anecdotes that will cheer you right up, allowing you to get on with your day in a more light-hearted manner. Great to pass on to your equally miserable colleagues and friends. You'll be known as the friend who always sends those funny emails and puts a smile on people's faces. No one need know where you got them from, and you can keep referring back on a daily basis as the site is updated, so you'll never run out of new material.

http://www.comedycorner.org

★ ★

:: THE FUNNY NAMES SERVER

Most people find it hard to keep a straight face when being introduced to someone new to find out their name resembles something funny like Ivor Biggen. The Funny Names Server has recognised the humour in people's and business names and has done all the hard work for you. Its compilers have gone through phone books and picked out all the comical ones for you to browse through and chuckle at. Read the top five for the best of the day, or browse through the whole server at your leisure. But remember: these are real people who have to live with these names for ever, and it's not nice to laugh at their misfortunes even if they are called Rainey Bowels.

http://www.funnyname.com

★ ★

:: THE REFLEX TESTER

When was the last time you tested your reflexes? Possibly when faced by oncoming traffic or when trying to avoid being hit in the head by an oncoming ball of paper from an overconfident work colleague trying to lob their rubbish in the waste bin? The Reflex Tester has been devised to prove all you fast movers wrong. All you have to do is press two buttons, one to start the reflex test and the other to stop it. Sounds easy, but you'll be surprised at how slow your reflexes are at first and you'll end up spending quite a bit of time trying to beat your own score. You will improve with practice, so don't give up. My personal best is 0.18 seconds, but I had to be dragged away from the screen – seriously addictive stuff.

http://www.happyhub.com/network/reflex

★ ★

:: VIRTUAL FAG BREAK

With the smoking ban in enclosed areas here in the UK, smokers all around the country are finding it virtually impossible to have a cheeky fag break, and that's not due to lack of opportunities to sneak off, more like lack of places to have a smoke legally. This website has come up with the perfect solution that will not only give you somewhere to puff away legally while indoors, but will also increase your health by stopping you from inhaling nicotine. Virtual Fag Break allows you to take a break from work, whether you smoke or not, to enable you to do something else less detrimental to your health. These guys are trying to highlight the amount of time smokers get away with having breaks, so VFAG have devised this creative little screensaver so that all can enjoy the free breaks but without the next-morning phlegm.

http://www.vfag.co.uk

★ ★

:: MUSEUM OF HOAXES

Are you one of those people who love getting on their friends' nerves by constantly pulling pranks on them? Or maybe you are seeking revenge in some way and need some ideas to get them back. The Museum of Hoaxes is the number-one site for all your prank ideas. Read through the library of hoaxes dating back hundreds of years, or get some inspiration from renowned pranksters – college students.

http://www.museumofhoaxes.com

★ ★

:: WHO THE F*** IS ALICE?

This website promotes the development and adoption of ALICE (Artificial Intelligence Foundation) and AIML (artificial-intelligence mark-up language). What this site offers its members is the opportunity to learn a simple language, making it possible to create their own robot that lives inside their computers. Chat online to the website's creation, Alice, but be warned: this chick has an answer for everything and won't put up with anyone trying to outsmart her. Technology heads will be in their element, while everyone else will just have fun trying to wind up Alice.

http://www.alicebot.org

★ ★

TRAVEL AND TOURISM

ONE OF THE first places people go to research their holiday plans is on the Internet. Whether it's to check up-to-date travel information or holiday destinations, the Net is the most accessible port of call when it comes to current information on travel and tourism. This chapter aims to give you a slightly different insight into the world of travel by highlighting all the weird and wacky places to visit, activities to keep you occupied and places to rest your head. Find out about strange customs and traditions from other countries as well as travel enthusiasts and what they can offer you. Take a look at the planet in a completely different way and realise just how weird our world really is.

:: SLEEPING IN AIRPORTS

For many travellers, delays at airports seem inevitable these days, so, whether you are travelling short- or long-haul, alone or with the family, it's a good idea to know the best places in the world's airports where you can lay down your weary head and get a few hours' sleep – for free! This site provides the budget traveller with the low-down on cosy corners, including comfort ratings and parking facilities. With more than 4,000 entries at 700 locations ranging from bus stations to waiting lounges, it ensures you need never book a hotel room again!

http://www.sleepinginairports.net

★ ★

:: AIR–SICKNESS BAGS

You can tell a lot about an airline's image from their air-sickness bags. Some barf bags are no more than a baggie with a twist tie, while other sickness bags could win international design competitions. Who cares? I hear you cry. Well, apparently some people do. This website is created by Swedish engineer and avid barf-bag collector Rune Tapper, and hosts the number-one resource for all your belch-bag research. Through many years of donations and personal travel, Tapper has amalgamated a whopping 1,070 different bags from 131 countries, and the numbers are ever growing! View them all in this comprehensive user-friendly library of unused puke packets that are searchable either by airline or country. Will he ever stop? What could possibly be next? How about Space Spew Sacks – one small step for mankind, one giant leap for Rune Tapper.

http://www.sicksack.com

★ ★

:: BED JUMPING

I must have lost count over the years during my childhood of the number of times I was told off by an adult for jumping on the bed. But it was so much fun, and not realising the consequences of either sleeping in a broken bed or having to pay to replace it, I felt it most unfair of grown-ups to spoil my enjoyment. This site is dedicated to this favourite naughty pastime and includes pictures and stories of bed jumping around the world while in the perfectly safe surroundings of a hotel. No need to worry about breaking the bed: they've got loads. Besides, you've paid for that bed, so you'll bloody well jump on it! More importantly, though, you can bounce to your heart's content, since there are no adults telling you off – unless you go away with the olds, in which case I suggest you make sure your room is well away from theirs.

http://www.hotelsbycity.net/blog/bed-jump

★ ★

:: AIR DISASTERS

Not exactly a joyful site unless seeing planes fall out of the sky and combusting into a ball of flames leaving hundreds dead is your idea of entertainment. This website is more of an air-disaster news and reference page, where people can come and get up-to-date information about air incidents from around the world. Heavily relied upon by the media for factual information, this is a no-joke site and they pride themselves on the accurate research that has been carried out by their team since 1996. Browse through the decades of archives, witnessing every type of air disaster from the lucky ones, from which people got out alive, to the fatal ones, whose victims had no chance of survival. Cutting-edge images and a strong source of information definitely make this a site worth visiting.

http://www.airdisaster.com

★ ★

:: EARTHCAM

Have you always longed to go travelling but never have the time or money to take the plunge? This website allows you to travel the world for free, and you can fit it all into one morning! OK, so it's not the same as physically being in these countries, but it's as near as you're going to get at the moment, so you can't really complain. Why not join in on the action and link up your webcam to the site so the world can see the area you live in, breaking down cultural barriers everywhere. Not sure if this site would be more suited to voyeurs rather than travellers – well, whatever floats your boat.

http://www.earthcam.com

★ ★

:: URBAN EXPLORATION

This site takes you places that have long been forgotten by society, making them even more tempting to visit. Take a virtual trip through disused buildings, drains and utility tunnels that are technically out of bounds to the public and witness many interesting pictures and findings along the way. The site has been running for many years now and its explorers dedicate their time to hunting down abandoned landmarks to appear on the site and in their publication, *Access All*

Areas: a user's guide to the art of urban exploration. Leaving no stone unturned, they plummet readers into a forgotten world of adventure and high risk, awakening the past into the future for all to see.

http://www.infiltration.org

★ ★

:: DO NOT ENTER

Enter the site of the DO NOT ENTER command. These signpost enthusiasts have taken it upon themselves to research the diverse variations of the most common road sign. Find out what the sign looks like in different countries around the world and see if you can spot your own from the bunch. Bored yet? Don't be – the site creators have expanded their signpost content to other commands, too. Browse through some more straightforward road instructions as well as the unusual and supposedly humorous ones. Personally, I'd take the advice given on the homepage and move on.

http://www.donotenter.com

★ ★

:: RUDE PLACES

Have you ever been on a road trip and stumbled across a place with a funny name that makes you chuckle so much you have to draw it to the attention of those travelling with you? This site has gone one step further with an alphabetical listing of places around the world with names that will make you giggle like a girl. The site creators are pretty certain that they have included all the best ones but I guess humour is a very individualised response, so there may be more to be found. A great way of curing boredom. I remember blankly gazing at a wall map when I was supposed to be cold-calling people for research purposes of the marketing kind. Ah, those were the days!

http://www.i-r-genius.com/rudeplaces.html

★ ★

:: WORLD LICENCE PLATES

Are you a vehicle-licence-plate enthusiast and always the first to understand how new systems work? What if you could learn about the different types of plates from around the world? This site is your ultimate guide to the history and origins of number plates. Search through continents and countries to get a comprehensive breakdown about each country and its plates. Get all the latest news and updates from around the world, as the site updates itself on a regular basis. Now all you have to do is pray that you get questioned about it in the pub quiz, because I can't think of any other time you'd need so much information on the subject.

http://www.worldlicenseplates.com

★ ★

:: MILE–HIGH CLUB

This is the official website of the infamous club of sexual air acrobatics. For years now passengers have been taking to the skies and using the air-travel experience as a perfect opportunity for a bit of high-rise fornication. Some blame it on the altitude or the lack of in-flight entertainment, while others are just sexual deviants who are addicted to the thrill of it all or who simply need another unusual place to tick off their hit list. For those who have yet to become a member, browse this site for information about how to join the club and guidelines that will ensure you a very bumpy ride.

http://www.milehighclub.com

★ ★

:: NOBODY THERE

A very eerie site that takes a look at derelict buildings around the UK. With very little text, the site runs as a photo library of multiple images from empty properties including hospitals, asylums, churches and other such public buildings. The site would be complete with a brief history or description on each of the buildings and possible location details just to set the scene if anything, but on the flipside the pictures leave the building's spooky story up to the imagination of its viewer, making the images all the more creepy.

http://www.nobodythere.co.uk

★ ★

:: PAYPHONE PROJECT

This website has everything you ever wanted to know about public payphones. What started out as a communication project, to see if people could randomly make friends by answering spontaneous anonymous calls from public payphones, eventually went out of the window, as incoming calls to many public phones in the USA were stopped or redirected to a main switchboard. The site has now taken on a different movement, still pursuing the initial subject of the phone booth, but with a more general approach to the subject. Read up on shocking news stories surrounding these seedy hideouts and view images of them from around the world. And, if that's not enough, you can be redirected back to our friends at EarthCam.com and watch them live in action.

http://www.payphone-project.com

★ ★

:: STATUE MOLESTERS

What better way to express your sexual desires than to hone your hormones with an unsuspecting statue? That's what the guys at Statue Molesters promote, and, while I'm not too comfortable with the context of the second word in that title, it makes for a very entertaining site. Finger (sorry) through the gallery of ardent gropers in action with their chosen statues from around the world, and then sift through your photo albums in search of that drunken holiday snap that would be right at home here. Admittedly, we've all had a grope. I've even got an old picture of my late granddad with his hand cheekily placed on the naked bottom of a statue, of which my grandma, who is posing with him, was blissfully unaware – bless 'em!

http://www.statuemolesters.com

★ ★

:: CURIOUS CUSTOMS

We Brits are supposedly reserved individuals who are well mannered and do all things proper. And, although we like to let our hair down now and again, we are expected to follow social-etiquette laws to portray our country in a dignified way. So I nearly choked on my tea and cucumber sandwiches when I stumbled across the website of a junior school in Kent dedicating an entire page to British citizens taking part in all manner of tomfoolery, including bread-and-cheese throwing, tar-barrel burning and something known as Bacup Nutters Dancing. What would Her Royal Highness make of all this?

http://www.woodlands-junior.kent.sch.uk/customs/
curious/index.htm

★ ★

:: UNUSUAL LIFE

This site is run by creative real-estate enthusiast Marlow Harris, who combines her passion for art with her real-estate expertise, resulting in some very eccentric properties. Harris has chosen a select few unusual homes from around the world and displayed them on her site along with various pieces of kitsch furniture and artwork. Expect to see some offbeat accommodations in some strange places, since there is no limit to how wacky this lady can be. My personal favourites are the Tiger's Nest Monastery, which is perched on the edge of a cliff in Bhutan, and the Christmas tree made from Mountain Dew cans. Get some great inspiration from this site, proving that it's possible to build the house of your dreams no matter how unusual your ideas are – just don't forget to consult the neighbours first.

http://www.unusuallife.com

★ ★

:: WEDDING TRADITIONS

Are you planning on tying the knot and looking for the perfect theme for your wedding? This site brings you wedding traditions from around the world and allows you to acquire inspiration from a choice of different cultures. Have the very best of everything with a pick-and-mix wedding tailor-made for you and your partner; or, if you simply want to make sure that you are sticking to the traditions of your own ethnic origin, you can use this site as a reference.

http://www.worldweddingtraditions.com

★ ★

:: DERELICT LONDON

Take a look at the nation's capital as you've never seen it before. This website will take you on a journey through all the forgotten places around London that were once bursting with life but now stand derelict like empty shells. Also included are interpretations of a vacant city in the form of people, places and tourist attractions captured by amateur photographer Paul Talling. The site depicts a seemingly hidden side to the city that often goes unnoticed by capturing things that we often overlook. Some stunning shots unlock the history of a London that has long been forgotten.

http://www.derelictlondon.com

★ ★

:: GHOST TOWNS

Visit some of the most famous towns that time forgot in these websites dedicated to ghost towns. Between the two sites you are able to view images and learn the history of unused towns across the USA, as well as signing up for tours and exchange travel tips with other enthusiasts in the online forums. Get all the latest news and updates and purchase memorabilia of your favourite ghost town. Ironically, these places are more popular for not being populated, as it's the silence that runs through each town that attracts people back by the masses.

http://www.ghosttowns.com
http://www.ghosttowngallery.com

★ ★

:: ROADSIDE AMERICA

This is your online guide to all the weird and wonderful places to visit in the USA. With so many offbeat tourist attractions to see, you'd be hard pushed to visit them all in one trip, so this site was created to enable you to get the experience online before deciding on where to visit first. No trip would be complete, however, without at least one sighting of a shoe tree. These trees stand proud (and rather smelly) around the country engulfed in second-hand shoes that have been added by locals, travellers and tree-shoe enthusiasts for years. At first glance, these trees can be mistaken for something that's housing a flock of birds, much to the astonishment of passers-by when they realise that they are in fact old shoes. Read the stories on how the craze started and get to know about many other equally strange American attractions.

http://www.roadsideamerica.com

★ ★

:: STRANGE BRITAIN

Britain is not outwardly recognised for being a strange nation, but this website argues otherwise and delves deep into a bonkers Britain. Find out about traditions, legends, ghosts and folklore depicting the unusual goings-on up and down the country. With many virtually unheard-of customs that may even come as a surprise to Brits themselves, this site is crammed with strange tales of past and present. My favourite is the day of no news when in 1822 the *Hampshire Chronicle* filled its pages with advertisements because it couldn't find any news to report on. Remarkably, the paper is still in print today, and is recognised as the country's oldest newspaper, dating back to 1772. Get this story and more in this truly patriotic site dedicated to bringing its visitors eccentric pastimes from a nutty nation.

http://www.strangebritain.co.uk

★ ★

THE HUMAN BODY

THIS CHAPTER TAKES a look at the human body and gives it a good dissecting, revealing all the obscurities and strange things related to it. We are all unique in our makeup and what is ugly to one person can be beautiful to another. This site will touch on appearance, bodily functions, body parts and a whole host of other human biological connections that have been highlighted in one weird way or another. Prepare to be shocked, sickened and possibly even turned on in this head-to-toe look at the human body.

:: AWFUL PLASTIC SURGERY

Eyes, ears, lips and hips all come in for the chop on this site in a brutal guide of how not to look as we plunge ourselves into the sinister world of awful plastic surgery. We all know that celebrities are the worst for going under the knife and some are now more famous for their mangled faces than for the art that brought them into the spotlight. Within this site you will witness the dramatic before and after pictures that show the less-than-flattering results of your best-loved celebs as well as the general public who put their trust in their surgeon and ended up like a character from Michael Jackson's *Thriller*.

http://www.awfulplasticsurgery.com

★ ★

:: MESSAGES IN BLOOD

Ooh, this will get you going. If you want to send an email to someone they'll never forget, do it in blood. This site provides the vintage wallpaper and the severed finger from which the blood oozes as you script out your message. You can even check out the last twenty 'writes' sent by others. Definitely not the kind of messaging service to use on Valentine's Day, unless of course you're into the whole say-it-with-blood craze that actress Angelina Jolie went through while dating her ex-lover Billy Bob Thornton – Google 'Angelina Jolie blood' and you'll get the idea!

http://www.bloodyfingermail.com

★ ★

:: THE BONY CHAPEL

If it's bones you're in to, look no further than this site. Lovingly put together by travel enthusiast Frisco Ramirez, it pays homage to a chapel decorated with the skeletal remains of the human body. The Sedlec Ossuary (a.k.a. Kostnice) is a small Christian chapel situated in the Czech town Kutná Hora, and, until Ramirez visited the church back in 1996, there was no reference to it on the Net. Within this site you can read through the history of how the chapel came about as well as opening times in case you are planning a visit.

http://www.ludd.luth.se/~silver_p/kutna.html

★ ★

:: BRAIN SURGERY

If you had fun dissecting frogs in your biology class at school and feel you are ready to move on to more complex projects, this site will take you through the online guide to brain surgery. Who said you have to be a doctor to perform such complicated operations?

After reading through this site, you'll have all the information you need to get you started on the task. Start off with the basic techniques, then, once you've fine-tuned your skills, you'll be able to move on to more difficult ones. Your first and most challenging job will be finding a consenting person to work on, which may take some doing! But fear not: the site also provides you with helpful hints on how to bag yourself a willing participant even if the practices are a little unethical.

http://www.lassie.demon.co.uk/scribb/brain.htm

★ ★

:: BALD R US

These guys aim to put a stop to balding men feeling inadequate because they have little or no hair. Bald and proud is their standpoint and they project it in many ways ranging from surveys proving that men who are thin on top are the best dressed and most romantic, to publicising horror stories of men who have dabbled in hairpieces and plugs. Are you a bald man? Before you do anything, take some time out to research this site thoroughly and realise that being bald does not make you less of a man and will, in fact, save you hundreds of pounds on hair products in the future. I'll leave you with my favourite quote from the site: 'God created a few perfect heads, and on the rest he put hair.' And there's plenty more where that came from.

http://www.baldrus.com

★ ★

:: DICKORATIONS

Does your pecker need perking up? Is it lacking that special something to catch the eyes of others? This is a fun site that might just have what you're looking for, and Durex condoms have come up with the solution – Dickorations. Dickorations are not to be mistaken for or used as a form of contraceptive but merely as a bit of fun and modesty for your middle man. Choose from a range of outfits that are downloadable from the site – simply print it out, cut it up, and attach it with the convenient belt latching system and you're good to go. With an outfit for every occasion, you'll never have to shop for your dinkle again.

http://www.durexdickerations.com

★ ★

:: FART PAGES

Love them or loathe them, we all do them, maybe not as prominently as others but we all, at some point in our lives, have passed wind. It's a natural release that the body sometimes experiences during digestion and, apart from the often heave-inducing smell, bottom burps are really quite harmless. This site salutes the fart, paying homage to it by listing sound bites of the noisy buggers in action. Select from various different genres, including noise, length and processor – even famous farts feature on this site. Personally, I see nothing wrong with a good old trump every now and again, and, as a wise man once told me, it's better out than in!

http://www.farts.netcarver.com

★ ★

:: THE G SPOT

Sex education at its finest with this funny animated description of how pregnancy happens. As I look back on my sex education at school, I think it was a little patchy. I'd get snippets of information from different lessons but no solid information that I could take away with me. It was almost as if the teachers wanted to address the subject without having to go into detail. No wonder so many of my old school friends got knocked up! This animation is fantastic and does all the explaining in an upfront way. Here's my advice to all schools out there struggling with the age-old debate about teaching kids proper sex education: sit the class

in front of a computer monitor and follow the link below
– job done!

http://websrvr4onj.audiovideoweb.com/avwebdsnjwebsrvr4
501/portal/media/media-050516-pregnancy.html

★ ★

:: LIFECAST

Kids grow up so quickly, so what better way to
preserve their youth than by taking moulds of their
tiny hands and feet as keepsakes? Lifecast is a
website that aims to do just this by specialising in
body casting. It is the number-one site for all you need
to know about the art. With a range of products, kits
and DVDs to get you started, you'll be mastering the
art in no time at all. Casting is suitable for the whole
body and with kits ranging from foot to face you can
personalise your house by displaying your body art in
many different ways. Watch out for those door knobs!

http://www.artmolds.com

★ ★

:: MONOBROW

Are you one of the rare people walking this earth who
have just one big eyebrow going across their forehead?
Have you been ostracised by society all your life because

of your apparent disfigurement and often think about reaching for the tweezers just to fit in with your peers? Well, don't! Before you start plucking, visit this site that promotes monobrow awareness, making the hairy caterpillar a normal facial feature that can be accepted by people whatever their brow count. Meet your monomaker in Brow of the Week or play the online game Monopoly. Never again will you feel like an outcast, hiding behind a hat or a fringe. If God had wanted you to have two, he wouldn't have given you one!

http://monobrow.com

★ ★

:: RATE MY POO

Poo enthusiasts worldwide have been visiting this site for many years because of its variety and freedom of speech surrounding the often taboo subject. For most, faecal matter is an unpleasant and unsightly product that we as humans come into contact with in one form or another on a daily basis, and we often take for granted its structure and form, dismissing the substance as nothing more than annoying waste that disrupts our daily duties. Rate My Poo is the only website where you are asked to give site members' brown stuff a good grilling, rating it from one to ten. Find out how your poo shapes up by uploading it to the site and letting others place their vote. A healthy, humorous and foul look at the variety of turds produced by our saintly bodies in the campaign to publicise poo-poo.

http://www.ratemypoo.com

★ ★

:: RATE MY MULLET

While in the mode of rating things, I thought I'd include this little gem that pays homage to the stylish 1980s hairdo the mullet. Read up on the history of the questionable phenomenon that spread like wildfire after football icons took to the fields sporting the much-talked-about style. Also spurred on by the glam-rock era, people from all walks of life were able to sport the hairstyle that was often described as 'business upfront, party in the back'. Much as with Rate My Poo, you are invited to browse through the pictures and rate them out of ten, and are also urged to send in your own mullet pictures to be judged. Students, don't be alarmed if you come across a picture of yourself. Apparently, this is the most common prank on campuses worldwide – so best sleep with one eye open from now on.

http://www.ratemymullet.com

★ ★

:: MUSEUM OF MENSTRUATION

This website is currently celebrating ten years of bringing its viewers information on menstruation throughout history. Scroll through the lengthy page of news, products and advertisements that have been used for various campaigns and educational purposes, making the ladies' hush-hush special secret into a common topic of conversation. Read through groundbreaking stories from a time when women weren't allowed to call their time of the month by its name, and how barriers have been broken over the years as women are now able to express themselves by talking about menstruation. All together now, after three, say '*Period!*' See. Nothing bad happened.

http://www.mum.org

★ ★

:: TALL CLUB

There is only one requirement you have to fulfil to be a member of this club and that is being tall. Now how tall do you have to be to be considered tall? I hear you ask. And the answer to that question I have yet to find out myself. So presumably anyone can blag themselves into this skyscrapers' club on the basis that they are tall compared with their surroundings. I myself am a mere five foot, but next to a group of five-year-old children I would be considered tall. So, even though the site developers' aim is to give practical and informative advice to lanky bods, they really should have thought through their prerequisite a bit more to stop short-arses like me from raining on their parade.

http://www.tallclub.co.uk

★ ★

:: FACE RECOGNITION

Are you always being mistaken for someone else? Or maybe you are constantly being told you look like someone famous. The clever technology at myheritage.com has a facial scanner that compares your features with those of celebrities, telling you whom you are most closely matched to. Simply upload a flattering picture of yourself to the site and in a matter of seconds it will carry out the process. Show off to all your friends your results, assuming, of course, you get matched with a good-looking A-lister.

http://www.myheritage.com/FP/Company/face-recognition.php

★ ★

:: NIGHT PEOPLE

Around sunrise, most people get up nice and early to get ready for work, and by the time their day is done they long to get tucked up in bed. What if your body clock were the completely opposite way round and the sight of daylight made you sleepy and want to go to bed, leaving the sound of hooting owls as your wake-up call at night. This site is dedicated to nocturnal beings highlighting the key elements that decipher whether you are indeed on the wrong time clock. A night person is someone whose natural body rhythms are more alert at night and slow down during the day. They are often seen as lazy by daytime people, so this site is the voice of night people and aims to give you a greater understanding of why they find night-time the best time to work. A must for people who love sleeping all day, and producing their best work at 2 a.m. Meet like-minded people and prove that you're not the lazy bum everyone thinks you are.

http://vic.com/~nlp/n-people.htm

★ ★

:: RECTAL FOREIGN BODIES

This site reports on the age-old problem of getting things stuck in your bottom. While some may be more familiar with the problem than others, there is no denying this is a widespread occurrence that has been going on for years. Visit this site for an in-depth look at case studies, images and tales of how foreign bodies end up the rectal area. Be amazed at the items found lodged up people's arseholes in normal households across the world, and learn how you can avoid being one of them. My advice is to check your seat before you sit down next time, or you might be in for a nasty surprise.

http://www.well.com/user/cynsa/newbutt.html

★ ★

:: KNOB SCAN

OK, so we've all done it: scanned in parts of our bodies at work when we think no one is looking. Hands, faces, breasts and bums. But this site isn't interested in these body parts. Instead, it invites you to send in your very best knob scans. Follow the how-to guide of scanning in your winkle safely and most effectively, or browse through the galleries to get some artistic inspiration. Don't have a knob? Grab a guy from the sales department: they're always up for making a prick of themselves.

http://www.nobscan.com

★ ★

CONSUMERISM

IN THE FAST-PACED world of technology, good old-fashioned 'going to the shops' is rapidly becoming a thing of the past. Most people would much rather shop from the comfort of their own homes and get their goods delivered straight to their door. In a world where near enough anything is obtainable and there's the technology to back it up, consumers are spending money like never before simply because they can. Retailers of today can, and will, sell anything over the Internet because there will always be one person tucked away in the corner of the world who has been searching for that very product or service. This chapter highlights some of these obscure products and services, giving you an insight into consumerism at its weirdest.

:: RENT MY CHILDREN

These are the websites of a marketing company claiming years of experience at finding the best way to rent out your son or daughter. Content includes client case studies, strategies and a free marketing evaluation. Birthday parties, prom dates, modelling assignments – the sky's the limit to the number of opportunities there are for someone to make use of your child. The most unadulterated marketing baloney you could wish for.

http://www.rentmydaughter.com
http://www.rentmyson.com

★ ★

:: ALIEN–ABDUCTION TAGS

Imagine yourself being whisked off into the galaxy by aliens. UFO sightings and alien abductions are on the rise. Will you return to tell the story? This site gives you the solution – alien-abduction dog tags on which your personal data and where you are from, the crucial data an extraterrestrial will need to get you back to your earthly origin – are die-stamped using a design based on NASA research for the Pioneer 10 Space Mission. You need never fear alien abduction again.

http://www.earthbounddog.com

★ ★

:: THE SAFEST BED IN THE WORLD

This is the ultimate in safe sleeping. The Quantum Sleeper bed comes equipped with protection against all kinds of natural disasters, including tornadoes, tsunamis, earthquakes and floods. It also protects against a biochemical attack and is bulletproof. Never again will you fear sleeping in the dark, or the things that go bump in the night. You'll sleep like a baby, having peace of mind that, no matter what is going on around you, nothing can harm you in your Quantum Sleeper. Optional extras include microwave oven, refrigerator and DVD player.

http://www.qsleeper.com

★ ★

:: 10K FOR A WIFE

Round up your single friends – we're all off on a trip! Successful entrepreneur Rod Barnett is a 41-year-old STD-free, eligible bachelor and is willing to pay $10,000 to the person who introduces him to the woman he proposes to – and she doesn't have to say yes! This guy is for real and luckily for us he is still single. In order to get the money, you have to recommend him to someone he proposes to. If he proposes to you yourself, he will donate the money to charity. After all, ladies, you won't need the money: you will get Rod himself.

http://www.10k4awife.com

★ ★

:: SPOOF ADS

Browse through the galleries of humorous adverts, based on real consumer brands. Some great adverts here, some for fun and others for political statements, but all with a message to be portrayed. This site is a link from the Adbusters main site, where you can find their online magazine, also called *Adbusters*, which is a non-profit publication based in Canada. Through their magazine, they aim to inform people about the erosion of our physical and cultural environments by commercial forces. Whatever your views, this is an interesting site with some thought-provoking content.

http://adbusters.org/spoofads/index.php

★ ★

:: SAUCY NOVELTIES

Planning a naughty night in? Or maybe you want to give your lover something they will never forget. Saucy Novelties provide you with all you need in the way of kinky treats to spice up your love life. Everything from

Rude Food to Saucy Toys, you're spoilt for choice when it comes to these tantalising treats. Just be careful around the willy soap lads!

http://www.saucynovelties.co.uk

★ ★

:: GRAB A GHOUL

It's Hallowe'en every day on this website and to prove it they dedicate their time to producing the most gruesome costumes imaginable. In these get-ups, you'll be the most avoided person at a fancy-dress party, since guests will be hard-pressed to know who it is under the disguise, or whether it is a disguise at all! The prices are very reasonable considering what you would normally pay for a costume of lesser quality and half the creative flair. See how they are made, or request a custom-made mask designed especially for you. Even the sickest of minds will be quaking in their boots. Mwahaha!

http://www.bumpinthenightproductions.com/

★ ★

:: ARE YOU CRAVING ATTENTION?

Have you always craved attention? Love to be in the limelight and hate going unnoticed? Well, this website has come up with the perfect concept for you. These people will create the illusion of an accident that will happen to you, and will tailor-make a life plan for you to continue on as if this accident really took place. Read through the cases of people who have had their lives fulfilled by these alleged 'accidents' and go through the five steps to changing your past and, as a result, your future. Mad? It's downright bonkers!

http://www.by-accident.com

★ ★

:: DEAD ROSES

Looking for the perfect everlasting gift for a loved one? Want to show your love through flowers? Send someone you love a bunch of *dead* roses. Order your bouquet online and show someone you care. Choose traditional red roses, or for the more romantic you can send black silk roses. At least your loved one won't ever have to worry about their dying. My only concern is the price!

http://www.deadroses.com

★ ★

:: POOP CALENDAR

Yes, you heard correctly. Monthly Doos is a website that is host to an annual calendar creatively depicting faeces in various situations. Now you would think that a calendar like this would be hard to flog, but the website sells out of the next year's calendar by October, so there are more poop perverts out there than we think! But fear not: you can view the calendar online along with plenty of other lovely turd treats for you to get your mitts on. How about some yummy chocolate doo drops, kindly gift-wrapped and ready to eat? Or Yule doos to decorate the tree with. It's poop like you've never seen it before, and is a celebration of what a load of crap we really are all full of. My personal favourite is December.

http://www.monthlydoos.com

★ ★

:: PORTABLE RESTROOM CLEANING SYSTEM

This little beauty is the answer to all your public-toilet-cleaning prayers, the Gamajet 9. It's the most advance toilet-cleaning apparatus of it kind. No need to scrub again, or suffer that backsplash you are accustomed to when faced with the force of water spraying back all the remains. This really will cut your workload in half, not to mention increase your lifespan by preventing diseases. So now you can have peace of mind that the job gets done and you stay dry, all the while maintaining a happy, healthy and sparkly clean bog.

http://www.gamajet.com/cleaning/portapotty.html

★ ★

:: BLENDER PHONE

Have you always dreamed of owning a kitchen appliance that operates all by itself? Or maybe you've always longed to possess a double-functioning kitchen device. Well, fear not, because I've found the site that will fulfil your dreams. The Blender Phone by designer Tom Myers. Although not a treat to look at, it works as a multi-functioning device by blending food as it rings, and is fully functional as a telephone or a blender. I thought I'd seen it all!

http://www.cycoactive.com//blender

★ ★

:: 20TH–CENTURY CASTLES

Calling all property developers: have I found an investment for *you*! Are you looking for a different kind of property like no other, something that can withstand a nuclear attack, and natural disasters? Well, 20th-Century Castles can offer you that property in the form of a missile base. But you've got to be quick: there are very few left, as they are selling fast — and with no plans to have any more built, it's an investment that will grow and grow. Meet Ed and Dianna Peden, the current company managers. Let them guide you through their very own transformed 20th-Century Castle, which has now been developed into their home and office. A claustrophobic's nightmare, an agoraphobic's dream!

http://www.missilebases.com

★ ★

:: NAVY SEALS

Pump up and kick ass with the Navy Seals workout DVD and video collection. Learn from the navy masters how to become a better person through their alternative approach to survival. Educate yourself on how to fight like a man or how to get yourself out of a life-threatening situation, all under the guidance of seven serious professionals who know what it takes to be a fighter. Just don't get on their bad side. Did I mention it's a fabulous website?

http://www.navysealteams.com

★ ★

:: THE ERECTION COLLECTION

Ah, yes, this website will make you feel all warm and fuzzy inside – a lovable cuddly toy site for adults only. The Erection Collection is a group of soft-toy animals sporting rather generous erections – and they come complete with a naughty poem that best describes their characters. What their purpose is is down to the individual, but they are certainly a novelty to look at and are great as jovial gifts to friends and family. Just don't get them mixed up with the kids' presents under the tree!

http://www.pacifictrades.com

★ ★

:: THE HERO MACHINE

This website hosts the creative answer to anyone who has a vivid imagination but lacks physical artistic flair. The Hero Machine generator makes your fantasies a reality by transforming your imaginary friends into fully fledged animated characters. Create a whole new world with your new buddies and let your imagination run wild with the things that they can do.

http://www.heromachine.com

★ ★

:: MOON ESTATES

Fed up with your own planet and want to see the world from a different angle? Moon Estates is your key to owning land on another planet. For a mere £19.99 you could be the proud owner of your own acre of land on Mars, Venus or the moon. With each property purchased you will receive a deed, constitution, property map, mineral rights and a copy of the original declaration of ownership. You will also get the chance to own larger plots of land up to ten acres for a negotiable price. Today the moon, tomorrow the universe!

http://www.moonestates.com

★ ★

:: BILLYBOB TEETH

These comical fake teeth have been around for a while now but the website has a lot more to offer than just gammy gnashers. For those who are not aware, Billybob Teeth are novelty chompers that are used as a part of a costume for dressing up, or playing practical jokes on people. As seen in the gob of quirky film director Tim Burton, these gnashers come in many comical designs to suit all. For all you sick-joke-loving parents out there, they even come as cute dummies for your babies. Check out the rest of the site for other novelty gifts just as ugly, but just as brilliant.

http://www.billybobteeth.com

★ ★

:: UNIQUE GIFTS

Does the thought of birthdays and the holiday season get you excited at the prospect of finding your loved ones the perfect gift – but you like your prezzies to stand out from everyone else's and always like to come up with original ideas that no one else has thought of? This website is your saving grace. Browse through pages of strange but in some cases practical gifts that will have people talking for ages about them. Why not get your brother a unique bikini remote control or your granny a nap alarm that stops her falling asleep at the wheel? There's something for everyone here. I know where I'll be shopping this Christmas.

http://www.thingsyouneverknew.com

★ ★

:: RUDE T-SHIRTS

What better way of letting the world know how you feel than wearing a T-shirt that spells it out to them? Perhaps you are pissed off with someone, or want to get something off your chest. Well, these outspoken tops are designed for people like you. Browse through the designs and choose the one that best sums you up, and, if you can't find one that works for you, they invite you to send in your own design, and if it's used they will pay you with real money and a choice of ten T-shirts free of charge. Not bad, eh?

http://www.tshirthell.com

★ ★

:: WEB UNDIES

Grannies all over the world will be shocked to find out that they can now purchase their bloomers over the Internet. This is your one-stop comprehensive shop to everything meant to be worn under your clothes, and these guys have it all. There are plenty of styles to choose from for male and female, young and old. From the exhibitionist to the prudish, the comfortable to just plain dangerous, there is something here for everyone, whatever your taste and intentions.

http://www.webundies.com

★ ★

:: GOBLER TOYS

This website makes you want to jump right in on the

action, but unfortunately it's not real. Not only is this a made-up factory, but the toys are not real either. Click on the links to learn about the history of Gobler Toys and their complex design and product information. Make sure you watch the entertaining videos, too, to enhance the experience of Gobler Toys.

http://www.goblertoys.com

★ ★

:: WHERE THE DEAD LOVE TO SHOP

A website containing everything you could possibly want when you're dead. If you love to indulge yourself in the darker side of life and enjoy a good Internet bargain, then you've come to the right place. There is an A–Z of everything dark and sinister and all for sale at a fair old price. With a generous item breakdown for each of their products and clear pictures, too, this site excels in meeting the standards of its customers, even if most of them have croaked.

http://skeletonbone.com/?source=deathndementia

★ ★

:: THE WHIPS OF OZ

So are you looking for somewhere to purchase your apparatus? This website is packed with all things adventurous in the world of bedroom activities. All its products are of the highest quality for your unique pleasure. This really is your online bible to everything bondage and they can tailor-make your desires to suit all levels of intensity. So grab a whip and hold on tight, it's going to be a bumpy ride!

http://www.whipmakers.com

★ ★

:: WHO WOULD BUY THAT?

People come from far and wide to visit this website and witness auction oddities from all over the Net. These guys patrol the World Wide Web looking for the weirdest, wackiest Internet auction items and place them right here on their site for all to ogle over. If you are looking for something unique and bizarre but haven't got the time to shop around for it, try this site and you'll be amazed at the amount of crazy stuff they've actually managed to find. Or, if you are selling a weird item and want to get it maximum exposure, you can contact the team and ask them nicely to put it on their site. All the weirdness of the Web here.

http://www.whowouldbuythat.com

★ ★

:: STUPID

It says it in the name: a website containing things that are stupid. If you are constantly trawling the Net looking for sites that include novelty junk that you can impress your friends with, then I believe this will satisfy your requirements. With everything from foul-tasting candy to plasters that look like bacon strips, this is your one-stop online shop for all your wacky gift ideas.

http://www.stupid.com/index.html

★ ★

:: PATENTLY ABSURD

Are you one of those people who are bursting with ideas but don't know where to get themselves heard? Or maybe friends and family tease you about your vivid imagination, finding your inventions laughable. You may find some solace in this site. It's the home of totally absurd inventions that eccentric minds just like yours have thought up. Browse through the archive of ideas that have been on the site since 1997. You'll have hours of fun laughing your way through the unbelievably outrageous ideas of the human mind. For more tomfoolery like this, check out another site along the same lines.

http://www.patent.freeserve.co.uk
http://totallyabsurd.com

★ ★

CRIME AND PUNISHMENT

IF YOU ARE a law-abiding citizen, you may not think this chapter will apply to you. If you're simply here out of curiosity and to gain an insight into how the other half lives, well, don't be so sure. There's a lot here to tempt you into a world of crime, scams, cults and revenge and, with this information all too available, it will take a strong-willed person to come out of this chapter with a clean mind. You may even surprise yourself by finding out just how dodgy you really are in an online quiz, or continuing on through the book with a brand-new identity. But fear not: there will be a chance to redeem yourself at the end and educate others in the errors of your ways.

:: SHOPPING CART ABUSE

The top-ten shopping-trolley abusers are named and shamed on this site, which also offers a 12-step programme to help shopping-trolley abusers mend their sinful ways. Set up by the Centre for Prevention of Shopping Cart Abuse, the site is dedicated to preventing the pervasiveness of shopping-trolley abuse, at local, national and international level in the belief that abusers are trying to undermine fundamental pillars of society. The site helps individuals to understand this unspoken threat, to offer counsel to those who cause harm to trolleys, and sings the praises of the people who return these silver chariots to their supermarket homes.

http://www.shoppingcartabuse.com

★ ★

:: JACK THE RIPPER

A detailed casebook website all about the East End murderer Jack the Ripper. Take your mind back over a hundred years to 1888. It's the East End of London and, mysteriously, a number of prostitutes are found brutally murdered around the backstreets. This website gives a meticulous analysis into the world of the unsolved murderer who went by the name of Jack the Ripper.

http://www.casebook.org

★ ★

:: CRIME LIBRARY

Take a look through a world of madness and mayhem in the form of the Crime Library. Read up on the sickest of criminal minds from serial killers to sexual predators. Find out why they really carry out these crimes and what makes them tick. Learn about gangsters and outlaws, terrorists and spies and help give answers to unsolved mysteries. Or why not brighten up a loved one's day by sending them an e-card with their favourite serial killer on it? There really is something here for everyone.

http://www.crimelibrary.com

★ ★

:: DUMB LAWS

An utterly absurd website depicting the dumbest laws from around the world. You will have hours of entertainment reading through each country's wacky laws, and, while some are more believable than others, all give an informal but humorous insight into just how much people can get away with. My favourite dumb law for the United Kingdom is: 'Those wishing to purchase a television must also buy a licence.' Seriously, how dumb is this law?

http://www.dumblaws.com

★ ★

:: MEET AN INMATE

Are you looking for the love of your life? Can't find a mate in the outside world and are struggling to make new friends? Have so much love to give but just can't find the self-fulfilling way of channelling it all? Well, look no further than Meet an Inmate. This website puts you in contact with hundreds of people waiting for someone like you to come along and save them from a life filled with loneliness and despair. They are waiting for you to make contact and have all the time in the world to soak up your loving thoughts and messages. The only downfall is that you may have to wait a while before you can start your relationship in the outside world, so my advice is steer clear of the serial killers.

http://www.meet-an-inmate.com

★ ★

:: FACT

FACT, or Fight Against Coercive Tactics Network, are a group of former cult members who assist victims of cults, mind control, psychological coercion and fundamentalism. Factnet focuses on protecting minds from harm caused by all forms of mind control and unethical influence. They aim to support, counsel and give advice through their own experiences, and have an open-door policy to anyone who is affected by mind control by any means. This website has helped many people worldwide and continues to grow daily due to its vast knowledge and outspokenness on the subject.

http://www.factnet.org

★ ★

:: MUSEUM OF SCAMS AND FRAUDS

Quatloos.com is a public educational website maintained by Financial and Tax Fraud Education Associates. They are your online guide to everything scandalous in the name of scams and frauds. Learn about the most intelligent spoofs circulating on the Internet, the financial world and employment. Read through real scam letters that have been circulated to people, attempting to reel them into money-saving programmes by the use of clever sales techniques and selective wording. Then witness responses from real people who have fallen victim to one of the many scams. A must-see site for anyone who uses the Internet, post or telephone or has contact with other human beings on a regular basis.

http://www.quatloos.com

★ ★

:: REVENGE LADY

Let's face it, people are generally arseholes and will try to stitch you up at any given opportunity. OK, that's maybe slightly harsh, but what I'm getting at is that, when people go out of their way to make our lives hell, we all seek revenge in one form or another. Well, this is the type of site that, once you've found it, you'll bookmark and refer to it for ever more. Email in your problem and a revenge lady will come up with the ideal plot to get back at your enemy. A very resourceful site where you can scan through other people's revenge stories, including those of some well-known celebrities. Take the quiz or play the game, and, if you're feeling particularly mischievous, brighten up some smug bugger's day by sending them a revenge e-card, just to give them a taster of what's to come. Oh yes, revenge is sweet.

http://www.revengelady.com

★ ★

:: NINJAS

On entering this site you need to be brave enough to continue or risk getting deported to the Oprah Winfrey website. Once in, you will be faced with everything you always wanted to know about ninjas, but were too afraid to ask. It's the type of website that I would expect the controversial makers of *South Park* to host, but, just in case they're not the creative mind behind the site and it is in fact run by real-life ninjas, I'd just like to say what a thoroughly exceptional time I had browsing through the pages of weapons, clothing and advice on how to 'pump up' and I wouldn't want to hear a bad thing said about it. Please don't hurt me!

http://www.realultimatepower.net

★ ★

:: WHAT'S YOUR PRISON BITCH NAME?

If you're planning a trip to jail any time soon you'll need to be prepared to face the barrage of nicknames your fellow inmates might call you. To save time and prove your street cred, I've found a website where all you need to do is enter your real name and the online generator will crown you with your very own prison bitch name. A very simple, straightforward website with not much substance to it, but you'll find yourself on here for hours inputting all the names of your friends and family. I'm all set with my new inmate name 'Turd Burglar'. I wonder what I'll be best known for in the slammer.

http://www.prisonbitchname.com

★ ★

:: CRIME SCENE CLEAN-UP

Crime Scene Clean-up are a specialised team of professionals who are committed to helping people when tragedy strikes. Their objective is to compassionately, safely and discreetly to restore a crime scene back to a safe state, bringing as much normality back to an area or property where a crime, tragedy or death has taken place. This is the sort of website that you would never hope to make use of, but if disaster did strike in your home or workplace these guys would be the first people you'd call. Or should I say the second, after the emergency services.

http://www.crimeclean-up.com

★ ★

:: HOW DODGY ARE YOU?

An online crime sheet where you are forced to face your demons and own up to the errors of your ways. Are you really as innocent as you thought? Or could it be that the penny sweet you took as a child when you thought no one was looking is back to haunt you to prove what a corrupt citizen you really are? While filling out the form, learn about the crime you may or may not have committed and find out what the maximum penalty is and the severity of the offence. Don't worry: I've proof-tested it for you and I can assure you that they won't track you. Hold on, I've just got to get the door ...

http://www.thesite.org/flash/dodgy.html

★ ★

:: THE SMOKING GUN

This website brings you exclusive 100 per cent official documents using material obtained by government and law-enforcement sources. Read through a plethora of pending and closed cases to keep you up to date with the latest court action. Their sources are so powerful they have even managed to get their hands on international celebrities' concert-performance riders. This is definitely worth spending a few hours reading through. Who knew, for instance, that Jennifer Lopez loved the colour white? This site is filled with such intriguing titbits.

http://www.thesmokinggun.com

★ ★

ART

ART ON THE Internet is always going to be complex. Graphically, something can be beautiful and awe-inspiring, but ultimately is it brought about by technology. Does this make it any less artistic or is technology simply a different medium that an artist uses to create their work? Whatever your opinion, this chapter is crammed with arguments for and against my thoughts and includes interactive sites where you can show off your own skills. Visit artists' personal sites, where you can view everything from dead animals to paintings by bottoms. See, something for everyone!

:: RESTROOM GRAFFITI

No need to spend hours checking out the creative writing on the doors and walls of the nation's public conveniences. It's all here on one website. Latrinalia – the study of restroom graffiti – is a word allegedly coined by a Scotsman back in the 1960s as infinitely more preferable to 'shithouse scribbles'. This mind-boggling site has ten huge galleries of toilet scribbles from the downright vulgar and lewd to the most poetic and love-struck sonnets.

http://www.itsallinthehead.com

★ ★

:: EXPRESS YOURSELF

This is a site where you can really let yourself go creatively, and then show off your work to the world. Come here to let off steam by chucking a few paint buckets around, or, if someone's pissed you off, send them an obscene but obscure picture message and call it art. Maybe you need to get something off your chest, or are you just bored and need some light relief. Whatever your mood, this site is simple to use and is a lot of fun. And who knows? Maybe your work will get spotted.

http://artpad.art.com/artpad/painter

★ ★

:: BARCODE ART

This is the website of artist Scott Blake, who creates his art by using a multitude of different barcodes to create a bigger picture. Browse through his portrait gallery, where you will find a number of celebrity faces made up entirely of barcodes. The Madonna piece was made up of 107 different barcodes from the CDs of all her music to create one unique portrait of the artist herself. Other work includes barcode flip books, datascape collages and barcode tattoos. The most interesting part of this site is the 'science' bit, where Blake decodes the barcode by explaining how they are made up. Barcode art will bring a whole new meaning to the way you shop!

http://www.barcodeart.com

★ ★

:: BUTT ART

Arse printing is the brainchild of artist Stan Murmur, and he came up with the idea when he was asked to find an organic item to use as a stamp for his art class. His paintings now sell for hundreds of pounds and he has become a celebrity in his own right, often wearing disguises so that his clients from his professional life don't recognise him and get offended. He does cheat a little, though, and has admitted that his paintings are not entirely created by his rear end. The finer detail in his work is carried out by, in his words, 'whatever else that gets dangled into the paint'. I wonder what he could be referring to.

http://slingshot.to/buttart

★ ★

:: KITSCH

This website is an ode to everything kitsch that can be found in film, music, art or decor. Derived from the German word for trash, kitsch is seen by many to be highly fashionable in an often unobtainable way. It is very hard to get the right balance of trash versus beauty, which therefore makes it harder for people to portray fully the 'kitsch' lifestyle. This site goes through the history of kitsch within art and also has some fun pages where you can take part in a quiz and view some ironic pieces of artwork that make up the world of kitsch.

http://www.worldofkitsch.com

★ ★

:: DRUNKEN DRAWINGS

Now this site could be the answer to all drunk and emotional females' prayers. As a woman, I feel I can comment on this in confidence, as I have many a time carried out this shameful act. When we get drunk, no matter how much we try to stop ourselves, we always end up calling the ex. Not only do we call the ex, but we also engage in an incoherent ramble either about how great our lives are without them, or how we can't live without them. Either way, it is most definitely something that needs to be avoided at all costs, and I feel this website is the cure. Get in from a drunken night out and, somewhere between leaning over the toilet seat and getting into bed, quickly go online and get some inspiration from fellow drunk Alan, who puts his work up on the Net. He even gives out his MSN address, so, instead of harping on to the ex, you can bend Alan's ear while doodling yourself a drunken drawing. Genius – and it will save on the phone bill too!

http://www.drunkendrawings.com

★ ★

:: MELANCHOLY KITTIES

When you hear about dolls for adults, two types immediately spring to mind. The first is the sex kind (see 'Gender, Sex and Sexuality') and the second is the china kind, the ones that sit in the display cabinet of your aunt's 'best' room. Now the ones featured in this site don't really fall into either category. Well, I guess they could, but I wouldn't recommend it. These dolls are for the fashionistas and grown-up women who still fantasise about dressing-up dollies. These highly exclusive and sought-after dolls are almost impossible to get hold of – believe me, I've tried – and they all have a unique character and role within the melancholy family.

http://melancholykitties.com

★ ★

:: MR PICASSO HEAD

So do you fancy yourself as a modern cubist artist or are you are destined to show the world your portrait-painting skills? Well, this is the site for you. This is a fun drag-and-drop site where you will turn a blank canvas into a work of art. It's based on the works of Pablo Picasso, and you will either be enhancing or defacing the works of this 20th-century artist by putting your own artistic flare into practice. Once you are content with your work, you can save it to the gallery and email it to your parents to show them that you did pay attention in school, even if it was only in art class.

http://www.mrpicassohead.com

★ ★

:: SHOW US YOUR DISCS

This is a protest site for innocent people like you and me, who get inundated with CDs from a renowned computer company. If you are one of these unfortunate people and are looking to find a way to vent your anger, look no further. Their aim is to collect 1,000,000 of these CDs and send them back where they came from in a bid to stop this behaviour continuing. They also aim to show the company how they are potentially harming the environment with the distribution of unwanted materials. One way they are combating the latter issue is by urging their viewers to get creative with the CDs. Have a sneaky peak at the gallery for ideas on how you can dress up your home and save the environment at the same time.

http://www.nomoreaolcds.com

★ ★

:: PAPERCLIP ART

So you're at work and you're bored. You've checked your emails, read your MySpace comments, poked someone on Facebook and MSN Messenger is like a ghost town. Yearning for something to do other than get on with your job, you stumble across this website and realise that you don't actually need the computer to pass time. Look no further than your own desk. This site is created by artist

Justin Schlecter, who dedicates his time, when he's not running his web-service firm, to building sculptures out of office supplies. His medium of preference is paperclips, because he finds them to be 'very portable and inexpensive'. So there you have it. Get creative at work like Justin and you too could be running the show.

http://paperclipart.com

★ ★

:: FACE MUGS

This is the website of ceramist and master potter Ron Dahline. At first glance, my initial reaction to his work was that his creations were ugly and grotesque. Having looked through his gallery, I noticed a comical side to these characters and started to develop a liking to them. His work is full of expression, and, although it's not at all attractive to look at, you can't help but continue to look. Not really the sort of gift you'd get your granny, but a must-have feature somewhere in your household. Take a look through the gallery of exaggerated creatures based on something of this planet, be it human or animal, all of which look on the verge of coming to life. My personal favourite is the Republican Penis Nose Mug (swings to the right)!

http://rondeeclayworks.com

★ ★

:: DEAD BATTERIES

Whoever said you can't make art out of batteries? Check out these charged-up beauties. Customised batteries, decorated and ready to use with a selection of images to choose from. Vote online for your favourite design or just hang out in their bulletin room. Very cheap and guaranteed to work, but for practicality it's not really worth it. A good idea, though, if you want to spruce up your own AAs.

http://www.deadbatteries.com

★ ★

:: ART MEETS TECHNOLOGY

I wasn't sure which chapter to put this one in at first, but my decision to put it into 'Art' was purely down to its content and the way it made me feel. Special Defects is the personal experimental project and digital playground of Antonio Costa, and he uses the medium of technology to convey his work. Navigating around this site is very easy and straightforward once you find out how. It took me a while to discover it, but once you do there are lots of little hidden treasures. So I'll leave it for you to decide, is this art or technology?

http://www.specialdefects.com/v2

★ ★

:: BLOG GRAFFITI WALL

More than 600,000 people had visited this site when I looked in, and have left their mark by drawing a picture or leaving a message on the graffiti wall. They were then asked to save their details by giving a name and website link of their choice that they would like people to visit. Once saved, it is then added to the wall with the rest of the drawings, where it can be viewed by visitors to the site. A fun website where you can get creative while promoting yourself or your business, or just sending a message to the world.

http://blograffiti.com

★ ★

:: BRA BALL

When you were a kid, did you used to spend hours trying to create a giant ball out of elastic bands? Or maybe you're one of those people who collect elastic bands at work to make one of these balls. Most offices have at least one floating around. Well, this American artist, Emily Duff, took elastic-ball making to a whole new level by creating the first giant bra ball. The bra ball stands five feet tall, weighs more than 1,800 pounds and is made up of 18,085 bras. Within the bra ball, there are lots of hidden objects and letters that were collected over the time period it took to make. So the bra ball acts as a time capsule. The story behind the bra ball is a very interesting read, as are the events surrounding the project. The bra ball can now be viewed by the public at the American Visionary Art Museum, Maryland, USA.

http://www.braball.com

★ ★

:: ASCII ART

ASCII art is an image made up of computer characters. At its natural size, it looks like a jumble of different text and characters but when the image is shrunk it looks like a portrait of a face. Browse through the archives of celebrity portraits and try to guess who they are. The best way to get the true effect of ASCII art is to view it on a 21-foot monitor, stand as far back as possible and watch the celebrity come out of the screen. Now where can I get me one of those in a hurry?

http://www.asciibabes.com

★ ★

:: MUSEUM OF BAD ART

The Museum of Bad Art (MOBA) is the world's only museum dedicated to the collection, preservation, exhibition and celebration of bad art in all its forms.

MOBA was founded by Scott Wilson when he pulled a painting of an old lady in a field out of a pile of rubbish in Boston. The online museum has now gone on to acquire hundreds of pieces all considered to be bad art. View the creations online and judge for yourself. Submit work of your own or any hideous old pieces that may be lurking around your attic or cellar from many years ago, there's always at least one.

http://www.museumofbadart.org

★ ★

:: THE ONE MILLION MASTERPIECE

The One Million Masterpiece is the concept of Paul Fisher. The idea behind this site is to create one piece of art consisting of a million small pieces of art by people from all over the world and from all walks of life. The final masterpiece will be viewed in galleries around the world and, as a result, each person who contributed a piece of art within the masterpiece will become a published artist. You are asked to make a donation before creating your piece of art, as they are hoping to raise over £3,500,000 for global humanitarian and environmental charities. Get creative for a global cause.

http://www.theonemillionmasterpiece.com

★ ★

:: THE TOASTMAN

Maurice Bennett is renowned in his native New Zealand as being the Toastman. He builds entire pieces of art through the medium of toast, cooked at different stages to produce texture and tone to his final pieces. His works consist of abstract pieces as well as portrait and real-life replicas of items of clothing. He has recently branched out into using other types of food, unveiling his Eminem portrait made up entirely of 5,040 M&M chocolate sweets – yummy!

http://www.mauricebennett.co.nz

★ ★

:: PENCIL PAGES

Your online comprehensive guide to everything you ever wanted to know about pencils. Learn about different types of pencils, brands and uses. Or maybe you are interested in history or facts about our lead-poised pals. Browse through the pencil galleries and witness the largest pencil standing at 65 feet tall, or the oldest pencil of around 400 years old. Although pencils are not really my hot topic of choice when it comes to killing time, this site provided me with an enjoyable if not informative way of filling my day.

http://www.pencilpages.com

★ ★

:: UGLY DOLLS

This website contains morbid fine-art dolls, created by artist and alternative model Ugly Shyla. These dolls seriously live up to their name and are definitely not for children or the faint-hearted. Ugly presents us with her work, which varies from crippled female dolls to dolls of dead babies. Ugly Shyla is also a performance artist and is often booked for personal performances including her abortion act, in which she appears to remove one of her dolls from her womb. She has also been known to do the odd wedding and bar mitzvah, but you need to get in there fast, because she gets booked up quickly for this type of work – as I'm sure you can imagine.

http://www.uglyart.net

★ ★

:: VIRTUAL STREET REALITY

An amazing website brought to you by English artist Julian Beever. He brings streets to life with his larger-than-life images, and if viewed from the right angle they appear three-dimensional. Julian has stunned passers-by all around the world with his virtual street art and photos of his work can be viewed on this site.

http://www.rense.com/general67/street.htm

★ ★

:: SHE CALLS IT ART

Artist and taxidermist Sarina Brewer uses dead bodies of animals and rebirths them into art. Some may find the work that she does to be unethical, although none of the animals used for her work was killed for the purpose of being an art project. All animal components are recycled. She utilises salvaged road kill and discarded livestock, as well as the many animals donated to her from their previous owners after their demise. There are some pretty grotesque images on this site, so you have been warned, but, generally speaking, Sarina's work can be seen as the preservation of life in the form of art. You can decide for yourself.

http://www.customcreaturetaxidermy.com

★ ★

FOOD AND DRINK

FOOD AND DRINK is forever evolving. As people travel the globe, the local cuisine travels with them and as a result we are subconsciously being educated on different culinary traditions. Some sites here will shock you, others will make you sick, but most, if you're like me, will just make you hungry and even more experimental with what normally passes your lips. There's plenty here for you to sink your teeth into, so grab a spoon and prepare your bowels for this gastronomic trip through the world of food and drink.

:: OUTRAGEOUS RECIPES

Picture this, you're sitting in a restaurant that you have been brought to by your date and the waiter hands you the menu. You start to read it and something doesn't seem to be adding up: 'Hogs Head Soup, hot dogs in chocolate sauce, scrambled eggs and calves brains, dry-roasted worm and banana bread, all washed down with some cheese coffee.' You would think this was a joke, but, believe it or not, these are actually recipes created by real people who consider these dishes to be appetising. This website is dedicated to such people who have submitted their own culinary creations for the brave to consume. The most bizarre dishes in the universe can be found here and they are definitely not for those of a queasy disposition.

http://www.wildrecipes.com

★ ★

:: TOAST

If you though there was very little to know when it comes to toast, then think again. The Toast Shop has been a purveyor of the world's finest toast since 1857. This dedicated family-run business hand-toasts bread over open fires before dispatching its royal ranges of toast to your door for consumption. The ranges of toast on offer include the Balmoral, the Windsor, the

Buckingham and the Kensington, so you know you will be receiving the very best quality in toasted bread from these experts. Order your toast online and surprise someone with toast delivered to their door, or you can purchase gift vouchers online so the lucky recipient can order some at their convenience. Quality comes before all with these people, so never expect a burned piece of toast – cold, but never burned.

http://www.thetoastshop.co.uk

★ ★

:: MEAT HATS

Remembering the past, cherishing the present and celebrating the future of hats – made from meat. This website contains a photo gallery illustrating a veritable feast of meat hats throughout the ages and includes photographs sent in by its subscribers. Learn how to make a base-bull cap or a crown from pig's feet as well as details of upcoming meat-hat events. Meat hats really are taking the fashion world by storm, and contents of this site will prove this point. A different, yet creative way of drawing the fashion world together with the meat industry, though I don't expect the craze to take off with vegetarians.

http://www.hatsofmeat.com

★ ★

:: NINJA BURGERS

This website is home to the original ninja burger. Read through the online menu and choose from a range of different ninja-style burgers. There is even a kids' choice with a whole site dedicated entirely to them. Why order a ninja burger rather than a normal burger? I hear you ask. Well, it's simple. They aim to deliver the burger to you within half an hour. You don't even need to get off your seat to open the door, as they will let themselves in, and you also don't need to provide them with your address because they already have access to it. How do the burgers taste? I don't know. Surprisingly, I'm still waiting for mine – they must have got into an altercation along the way. God, I'm starving!

http://www.ninjaburger.com

★ ★

:: ARCHIPELAGO RESTAURANT

This is the website of a unique restaurant situated in the heart of London. Diners flock to this eatery due to its distinctive décor and mouth-watering menu. The team at Archipelago seek out the finest culinary influences from around the world and fuse them together with the exotic, the exciting and the unexpected. Expect your standard meal to look something like this:

STARTER: *Peacock on a date with tomato and vanilla confit.*

MAIN: *Sliced wildebeest fillet in a hot and sour sauce with nutty soba noodles.*

DESSERT: *Granadilla bavarois topped with twenty-four-carat gold and champagne glaze.*

Prices here are not cheap, but neither are their ingredients. I urge everyone to at least give it a go – you might just surprise yourself.

http://archipelago-restaurant.co.uk

★ ★

:: BAD COOKIE

We all look forward to finishing our Chinese meal and being presented with fortune cookies. Whether you see it as just a bit of fun or you really do believe that your fate will be decided once you read the little slip of paper, it's a nice traditional way of ending the meal among friends. Bad Cookie is a website that is really not for those who believe in the meaning of the message but for those cynical ones who think it's all a joke. A very straightforward site in which you simply open up your cookie to read your message of bad fortune. And, if you're feeling a bit naughty, you can send your own bad cookie to an unsuspecting friend and freak them out with truths that are very close to home. Don't worry: those who oppose this site have their chance to fight back by leaving their damning comments on the site. Also check out http://www.weirdfortunecookies.com for an equally amusing take on the psychic snack.

http://www.badcookie.com

★ ★

:: BROCCOLI MAN

Broccoli Man is currently taking the world by storm, spreading his message of nutrients and fibre to young and old. On this website you can witness his personal appearances in the form of newspaper and magazine articles, conferences, ball games and protest marches. Listen to radio interviews and live performances or watch clips from upcoming Broccoli Man videos. He is unstoppable and will go to great lengths to spread the message of his purpose to the world. All together now: 'Vitamins and fibre are good for you, so don't you want some broccoli? I know I do.'

http://www.madmartian.com/broc/index.html

★ ★

:: BUG EATING

Are you fed up with your staple diet of fruit, vegetables, fish and meat and are craving the unusual? Well, look no further than this site dedicated to the culinary delights of the insect world. View pictures of people's favourite dishes and the unsuspecting participants tasting the grubby concoctions. For all you hard-core bug samplers, this site will lead you to neighbouring websites that list recipes, facts and the option of signing up for the bug newsletter. You'll be spoiled for choice with the number of bugs in store, and, with well over a million different types of insect to choose from, you'll never lack variety in your diet again.

http://eat.bees.net

★ ★

:: MAD ABOUT CURRY?

You'll be hard pushed to find a Brit who doesn't like curry, so much so that over the years Asians have adapted their own recipes to cater for our tastes. Curry Mad is your online curry haven, where you can purchase gift vouchers for use at more than six hundred curry houses across the UK. Search for your local curry house and redeem your vouchers there – it's that simple. To make your experience on this site even more enjoyable, they have provided you with the curry game, which I might add is very entertaining, and a curry quiz to test your knowledge on your so-called passion. One word of advice: never visit this site on an empty stomach or you'll leave here broke and about two stone heavier.

http://www.currymad.co.uk

★ ★

:: DANS LE NOIR?

This is, without a doubt, the rarest dining experience you will ever find. Dans Le Noir is a London restaurant staffed by blind people, and the idea is that you eat your meal in total darkness. It's thought to enhance the flavour of the food and allow you to experience the taste to the fullest. You and your guests will be led through a succession of curtains until you are finally plummeted into darkness and escorted to your seat. The food served is an international modern cuisine, but to gain maximum effect from this experience it is advised that you choose the Surprise Menu, meaning you won't know what you are eating until you have consumed it, and even then you may still be questioning what it is.

http://www.danslenoir.com/london

★ ★

:: GROCERY LISTS

Do you leave your grocery list in the trolley following a shopping trip? You'll think again after visiting this website. This is the world's largest online collection of found grocery lists that people have discarded or thrown away. Now it may sound exceedingly boring, but you'll be intrigued and glued to your monitor once you start browsing through some of these lists. It's a bit like watching the so-called reality TV programme *Big Brother*, where you're not in the slightest bit interested in viewing these moronic people but you find yourself doing it anyway. Reading through what people consume in their own homes gives you a glimpse into their lives and I guess that's what the attraction is. A surprisingly entertaining site that has proved to be such a hit that the creators have had a book published with thousands of disused shopping lists for its readers to ogle. Check it out and see how long it takes before you can tear yourself away.

http://www.grocerylists.org

★ ★

:: RUDE FOOD

This is the adult playground for food that is rude. Browse through the well-organised, alphabetically listed pages of food brands that bear a naughty name. While some of these products are shrewdly named for marketing purposes, the majority here are down to naivety and language differences. You'll feel like a mischievous schoolkid again chuckling at words like 'bum bum' and 'fart drink'. A lot of research and picture hunting has definitely been put into this project and it's paid off, because the results are hysterical once you get into it. Best of all there is a breakdown of the product information, so you'll know how to look out for your favourites while holidaying abroad.

http://www.dazbert.co.uk/sites/rudefood

★ ★

:: I HATE CILANTRO

This website is for people who have a severe disliking of cilantro, more commonly known as coriander. Read through the cilantro horror stories and see what all the fuss is about, or sign up and get your chance to rant about it in the online forum. I didn't realise that a herb could cause so much offence. Now parsley I can understand – and don't get me started on thyme!

http://www.ihatecilantro.com

★ ★

:: I LOVE MARMITE

Well, they say you either love it or you hate it, but this site is a dedication to all those who love this yeast-extract spread. This is clearly a US site, so you'll probably find the 'What is Marmite?' page particularly amusing, and it makes you wonder why in fact Brits love the stuff. There's loads to do here in the name of Marmite: you can read up on recipes, find out about new products and even discover where in the world you can purchase the stuff so you'll never get caught short when abroad again. Personally, I don't love it or hate it, I just like it – they should have a category for nonchalant people like me.

http://www.ilovemarmite.com

★ ★

:: PORK FOR KIDS

This website is an educational site about pork. Kids can log on and learn all about where pigs come from, how they are grazed and finally what happens to them once they are slaughtered. This dressed-up fun site will teach kids about how to cook with pork and the best way to utilise your piggy. They even make personal trips to schools to preach about pork facts. These swine enthusiasts have put a lot of time and effort into this site and as much as I admire their passion for pork, it has to be said the show-and-tell section is just plain weird. I'm still struggling to see a real purpose behind this site and, personally, if the Internet had been around when I was a kid and I happened to stumble across this site, I think it would make me think twice before eating pork again – definitely weird.

http://www.pork4kids.com

★ ★

:: POTATO OF TERROR

Are you a budding writer with loads of potential but are extremely shy and reclusive? Do you yearn to share your writings with others so they can experience the gift that you have been bestowed, but don't want the fame and notoriety that comes with it? Take a leaf out of this anonymous poet's book and pretend you are a potato. Create a whole world around your character, giving yourself equally far-fetched friends such as carrots and other more obscure vegetables. No one need ever know your true identity but your character will become a legend. Network with other characters whose creators have done the same thing due to their wish for anonymity. There's a whole made-up world out there waiting for more unusual but gifted characters – so get started on creating yours.

http://members.tripod.com/~potato_of_terror/index.html

★ ★

:: THE TWINKIES PROJECT

This website was based on a study carried out in 1995 at Rice University in Houston, Texas. What these students aimed to do was determine the properties of a cream-filled doughnut, better known as a twinkie. On this site, you can bear witness to six different practical tests all carried out under strict regulations, and watch what happens when you cross a twinkie with science. Kids, don't try this at home, since it can prove to be very dangerous and utterly pointless. You've been warned.

http://www.twinkiesproject.com/index.html

★ ★

:: PEANUT BUTTER LOVERS

Warning! This website may contain traces of nuts. No, this is not some perverted peanut-butter-loving site: it's dedicated to people like me who can think of nothing better than a piping-hot fresh bread roll smothered so thick in peanut butter that you can't open your mouth to chew it. (Is your mouth watering yet?) Learn all about the history of the spread and how it's made, or sink your teeth into some yummy recipe ideas to further your passion for peanut butter. And don't forget that the whole of March is National Peanut Month, so get out your diaries and start preparing for how you're going to spend it.

http://www.peanutbutterlovers.com

★ ★

:: THE SECRET HISTORY OF THE FRENCH FRY

Something that I never thought I'd ever find myself needing to know is the origination of the French fry. Presumably some French dude just happened to stumble across the idea and it took off from there. Well, near enough true. This website contains the full secret history of the origins of the French fry in all its glory. The writer of the article, Debbie Stoller, takes us right back to the beginning of when the potato was founded right through to how they evolved into the fast-food fries they are today. Fascinating stuff here, I'm sure you'll agree.

http://www.stim.com/Stim-x/9.2/fries/fries-09.2.html

★ ★

:: THE CONDIMENT PACKET MUSEUM

The lengths that people will go to in their search for collecting items of interest will always astound me. Within this very neatly presented website is page upon page of meticulously lined-up condiment packets of many different varieties. The little sachets are displayed according to age, product or content, and you'll be hard pushed to name one they haven't got. If this isn't enough to satisfy your condiment needs, visit their neighbouring sites containing more information about yet more condiments and the like. Strangely, they have an online store, which you would imagine sells condiments, but, to my disappointment, not a sachet in sight! Instead, it sells souvenirs from the site in the form of T-shirts, badges and mugs. Barmy!

http://www.clearfour.com/condiment

★ ★

:: JAPANESE PIZZA

If the thought of Japanese pizza is enough to put you off your chicken teriyaki, then maybe you shouldn't read on. This website claims to be the first Japanese pizza page and lists all the different toppings that are on offer. At first glance, they don't look any different from your average pizza, and their names seem pretty harmless, too, but on closer inspection you'll find they use some very questionable toppings. The first one to catch my eye was smoked salmon – not unheard of, but not my first choice of pizza topping. Next we have mayonnaise and potato, which I guess some would say could be an interesting accompaniment to pizza. However, not really my cup of tea. And then we have squid ink used instead of tomato sauce, which apparently stains your mouth black for that authentic 'I've just eaten a pizza' look – nice!

http://www.chachich.com/mdchachi/jpizza.html

★ ★

:: THE FOOD MUSEUM

This website is the ultimate online guide to all manner of culinary subjects. The site is host to many different exhibits from around the world, highlighting the diversity in diet between cultures. The Food Museum also provides its visitors with various educational outlets dealing with diet, nutrition and news, enabling the site to grow in population as a result of this. If food is your forte, you'll love this site and will find yourself referring back to it from time to time. A real eye opener to the diverse world of food, it will not only educate you but will also make you rather peckish.

http://www.foodmuseum.com

★ ★

:: WEIRD MEAT

Just the name alone is enough to make your stomach churn and the website definitely lives up to its title. This is the blog site of a hardcore traveller who dedicates his life to exploring the world of food. Not content with straightforward dishes that are common to most Westerners, he would much rather find out about delicacies that are virtually unheard of, or indeed thought to be inedible to many across the world. His aim is to explore what cultural differences there are between people's attitudes to food and why to one person grilled dog is an everyday dish, and to another it's like eating their oldest friend. This guy will and does try everything, as you will see from the pictures, breaking down barriers through the medium of food.

http://www.weirdmeat.com

★ ★

:: STRANGE BARS

This website is the home of barflies all over the world. Many strange US waterholes are featured on this site depicting weird tales of drunken encounters with their locals and other strays that pass through their doors. You are invited to complete the site's mission to 'hang with drunks' and register yourself on the online community of your fellow barfly. Strictly for the hardcore liquor lover, this site acts as your guide to the quirkiest bars around, where you can chat to like-minded people and exchange your tales of drunken debauchery.

http://www.strangebars.com

★ ★

GENDER, SEX AND SEXUALITY

THERE WILL ALWAYS be conflicting opinions when it comes to gender and sexuality issues, and, as long as people keep an open mind on the subject and respect that there are many different types of individuals with diverse needs and desires, the world can move forward in a more positive way. It is clear from this chapter that there will always be a battle of the sexes, but, as long it's taken lightly, we can all see the funny side of our own downfalls and imperfections. Sex is one of the leading industries on the WWW today, with more hits than any other sites. It's clear what's on the minds of most Web users!

I tried to steer away from the obvious porn sites (sorry lads, or ladies for that matter!), and instead include sites that aren't there for your sexual pleasures, but to inform, educate and entertain people on sexual subjects they may never have heard of. So, ice buckets at the ready, you are about to embark on the hormonally charged chapter that is 'Gender, Sex and Sexuality'.

:: TOILET TRAINING

This site has been put together by MAPSU – the radical Mothers Against Peeing Standing Up, an organisation who want to dispel once and for all any belief that men can pee accurately standing up. Peeing standing up destroys families, they say. Myths regarding the way men use toilets are vigorously dispelled and two great posters are provided online to put up in bathrooms to aid the campaign. A must for men who think they can pee through a doughnut from 40 feet.

http://www.mapsu.org

★ ★

:: FORGET–ME–NOT PANTIES

This is the ultimate purchase for men who have a need always to be in control of everything, including the whereabouts of the females in their lives. This amazing technology will enable men to keep track of where their wives, girlfriends and promiscuous daughters are at all times – and it's all in their knickers! Forget-me-not cotton panties come in a range of different styles, but the most important thing is that the tracking device is virtually invisible to the person wearing them, meaning they will have no idea they are being monitored. Start out with the basic design or splash out on the advanced model, which promises to monitor things like temperature and heart rate, so you'll know when it's time to move in on her. Buy these panties online as a gift for your unsuspecting loved one, but make sure you know what you're getting yourself into: you wouldn't want your controlling ways to come back on you!

http://www.forgetmenotpanties.com

★ ★

:: CONDOM NOVELTIES

This is your one-stop shop for everything condom-related. Choose from an enormous range and variety of condoms to suit all manner of tastes, or buy condom-related items as novel joke gifts for your testosterone-filled friends. There is something here for everyone to enjoy, and, since it's promoting safe sex, there's all the more reason to celebrate this site. Just make sure that, if you do decide to use any of these products, they carry the British Standard Kite Mark – well, you can't be too careful, can you?

http://www.condomnovelties.com

★ ★

:: DIARY OF A LONDON CALL GIRL

This is the blog of writer and call girl Belle de Jour. Her daily writings keep her readers updated with her whereabouts, experiences and general thoughts and opinions on her life as she knows it. With a succession of no fewer than four books under her belt and contributions to other publications as well as the occasional book review, this no-holds-barred writer is in no way shy about her profession and expresses it through the medium of writing. Visit her blog for an insight into a taboo lifestyle, or for a deeper delve follow the links to buy her books.

http://belledejour-uk.blogspot.com

★ ★

:: CHEATING HUSBANDS

Do you suspect your husband or partner of cheating but just can't quite get enough evidence together to string him up by his balls? Well, the professionals at Cheating Husbands are more than equipped to deal with your kind of problem. They provide you with a link that could potentially change your life, leading you to a site that provides you with the very best in spy software so you can track exactly what he gets up to online and who he's speaking to. The website also offers professional advice and support for sufferers of cheating partners and aims to build up your self-esteem again so you can face the world as a confident woman. Cheating Husbands is like the *First Wives Club* (Hugh Wilson, 1996) of the Net, kicking these cheating scumbags right where it hurts. Girl power and all that jazz – those Spice Girls would be proud.

http://www.cheating-husbands.com

★ ★

:: THE COST OF SEX

Have you ever wondered just how much having sex with your girlfriend or partner is actually costing you? You'll be shocked to find out that keeping your sex life active is in actual fact bleeding you dry of all your hard-earned cash. Visit this website to work out how much sex is costing you. Be sure to forward this link to all your friends to stop them breaking the bank, too. Now you'd think that, after males all around the world have been shocked with this stomach-churning reality, they would provide some kind of aftercare support and advice. But no: you are just left with the cold hard fact that you're being robbed of your money just to get your end away. It seems men really do go to great lengths for sex after all.

http://www.costofsex.com

★ ★

:: DEVIANT DESIRES

This website, created by author Katherine Gates, is an online guide to deviant desires and hosts a sexual library of all things kinky in the world of temptation. Designed not to turn you on, but to be used as a source of education and research with like-minded people, the site will open your eyes to what many consider to be perverse but is the norm in households worldwide. On entering the site, you are asked to take part in the kinky quiz – a kind of initiation into the website. Once you've completed the quiz, you are able to roam freely around the site's rooms, each depicting various types of sexual fetish, enabling you to gain a greater knowledge into the different desires of your fellow person. An open mind and plenty of cold showers are advised while you're viewing this site.

http://www.deviantdesires.com

★ ★

:: DISGRUNTLED HOUSEWIFE

This is the website of a modern-day mama and her daily reports on being a woman. She offers relationship advice, recipe ideas, yummy cocktails and food to keep a hold of your man. Although this all sounds very Martha Stewart-esqe, it's far from it.

The site is packed with feminist tones, appreciating the female body, putting down men in the form of the Dick List and inviting women to submit their secret desires while, in return, the hostess will tell hers. Women will feel right at home here and men will either be fascinated and amazed at the feminist content, or unsurprisingly find it very arousing and use it as another one of those sites to add to their favourites.

http://www.disgruntledhousewife.com

★ ★

:: DOGGING, ANYONE?

With UK laws on the sexual act of dogging being very ambiguous, it cannot be summed up in one sentence whether or not the act is illegal. Either way, Brits have been dabbling in the voyeuristic act for years now, and, with no sign of its slowing down, the people at Dogging Central have devised a website dedicated to this outdoor sport. With the majority of dogging being performed in cars, angling oneself can prove to be quite tricky. This site offers advice on which positions work best, and also ones to avoid. And if you're new to the game you can read through the ten commandments enabling you to get to grips with dogging etiquette to disguise the fact that you are an amateur. Definitely worth a look if you're planning a trip to the outdoors.

http://www.dogging-central.com

★ ★

:: BIKER MATCH

Are you looking for your perfect partner to bike off into the sunset with? Maybe you're after a cool rider in tight leather who's going to drive you wild with passion, or a speed demon who's the leader of the pack. If so, then let the folks at Biker Match take care of your dating dreams by finding you that perfect mate. Whether you are searching for a male or female, young or old, you are sure to run into your dream date by searching this site. Read through the success stories of other couples who have found love online and get yourself signed up to one of the many Biker Match events so that you don't miss out on all the top totty.

http://www.bikermatch.co.uk

★ ★

:: FURNITURE PORN

I have come to the conclusion that, when dealing with sex and people's desires, you must keep an open mind and try not to judge others for dabbling in sexual acts that may not appear to be the norm. But bookmarkers of this site are just downright wrong! Furniture Porn is a website that definitely lives up to its name. If you enjoy watching deckchairs getting it on, then this one's right up your street. Never again will I be able to veg out on my sofa without wondering what it gets up to with the armchair while I'm out doing the shopping. I guess everyone is entitled to a bit of happiness, but somehow I think these guys have gone too far.

http://www.furnitureporn.com

★ ★

:: GAY SQUARE DANCE CLUBS

Are you a homosexual male or female struggling to find your local square-dance club? I thought you were, so here's an entire association devoted exclusively to people like you looking for that square-dance release. The International Association of Gay Square Dance Clubs, or the IAGSDC to its creators, have been providing the gay and lesbian communities with square-dance information since 1983, and with no sign of the recreation slowing down they are ever expanding with groups in the USA, Canada and Japan. Create an online profile and be the first to share and receive your square-dance news in an environment where you can really be yourself.

http://www.iagsdc.org/main/common/index.php

★ ★

:: GIRL GEEKS

This website is a meeting place for women who love their information technology and don't want to share it with the boys. With specialist sections such as 'Career Advice', 'Girl Geek of the Week' and 'Women To Look Up To', this is a melting pot of hormonally charged females putting their mark on what is widely seen as a male-dominated area. An interesting site, admittedly, if not a little desperate. I'm all for women empowering themselves but feel the site could be far more hard-hitting if it's makers didn't keep stating the obvious fact that they are women who can use computers.

http://www.girlgeeks.org

★ ★

:: GOTHIC LOVE ONLINE

For those of you who are interested in pursuing love in a darker dimension and are struggling to find that outlet in your seriously mediocre life, this website could be your ticket out of Pleasantville. Gothic Love Online is host to personals for the dark and aims to put you in touch with your match, enabling you to fulfil your deepest desires. Create your own profile for your potential match to hunt you down. Or, if you can't wait for them to come to you, browse through the profiles already posted and see who takes your fancy. Be sure to keep me informed of any relationship development, as I will feel solely responsible and self-gratification is my medicine.

http://www.gothicloveonline.com

★ ★

:: HEARTLESS BITCHES

Men, here is your warning to stay as far away from this website as possible, because the females in here seriously don't want your kind hanging around. This site, which proudly stands for 'being in total control, honey!', welcomes you by showing you its manifesto. If you agree with most of the statements depicted on its list, then you've probably found somewhere you can call home. With hearts of steel, these Bitches go to great lengths to be heard and will in no way be keeping quiet about their solidarity when it comes to proving that they're not soft. Sisterhood at its strongest – and not an apron in site!

http://www.heartless-bitches.com

★ ★

:: HOW TO IMPRESS YOUR DATE

A humorous site with dating advice we all too often want to dismiss, because, let's face it, who needs to be told how to date? If you are, however, struggling with the 'getting past the first date' syndrome, you might want to pay attention to the free advice kindly doled out by this website. You'll be faced with a dating scenario and will get the chance to view how the couple get on in response to how they are behaving. Its aim is to get you on to that second date and expel all the hang-ups that people have surrounding dating. If you like this site, follow the links at the bottom of its page for advice on dancing and, more importantly, how to act convincingly.

http://www.zefrank.com/date_1/navigation.html

★ ★

:: PHALLIC MUSEUM

This website is dedicated to a man's best friend – his penis. Not very rich in content, but the subject matter is fairly odd to say the least. Have a poke around this site and see how you measure up on their size chart, or if in fact you have reached puberty at all. You may find the 'Mormons on Masturbation' text particularly helpful for those of you who simply can't leave it alone; or, for the more creative among you, take a look at the phallic-art section, where you will find work by artists who definitely let their manhood rule their minds.

http://www.phallic.org

★ ★

:: LADIES' WEAPONS

This is the website of Italian artist Antonio Riello. Worryingly, his obsession with firearms led him to give the manly weapons a fluffy makeover, turning them into fashion accessories for stylish women. Browse through the images for a more detailed view, all of them given their own unique names after various ladies. Also mentioned, but not featured, is high-protection armour to guard females against urban dangers. Never again will modern-day women have to worry about their machine gun matching their Manolo's. With plenty to choose from, you wouldn't want to piss these ladies off.

http://web.tiscalinet.it/ladiesweapons

★ ★

:: LADIES AGAINST FEMINISM

LAF are a group of Christian women who value their place in the home and do all that they can to lead a wholesome life in which their families come first. Unlike the attitude of most career-minded single women today, who will often put on hold settling down to a life of domestic bliss, theirs is to urge you to preserve and prepare yourself for your future husband by remaining pure physically, emotionally and mentally and by developing all the character and skills that a righteous young man will need in a wife. It has an interesting outlook on feminism, where some will be shocked by the opinions of these women, while others may feel right at home. I think I'll reserve my judgement on the subject for fear of any repercussions.

http://www.ladiesagainstfeminism.com

★ ★

:: OUCHY THE CLOWN

This is the website of bisexual adult clown Ouchy, for whom being a clown is a true lifestyle choice. Much more than just a circus act, Ouchy is a disc jockey, performing at all your parties and functions, a trained and certified meeting facilitator who will take on brainstorming sessions, conflict resolution and organisational development, and finally an experienced clown dominant, who specialises in: 'Bondage and discipline, Hot wax, Straight razor shaving, Boundary pushing and making you laugh while I hurt you'. This really is one of the most talented clowns on the Net, and, judging by the pictures in his gallery, a force not to be reckoned with. It's all a bit of harmless adult fun, though, isn't it?

http://www.ouchytheclown.com

★ ★

:: STUPID PENIS TRICKS

What started out with a fascination for her boyfriend's penis, independent woman L Michelle Johnson decided to collate different animated penises in varying costumes, characters and situations. Start by browsing through the pages to view all the penis pictures, or jump straight to 'the list', where you can pick out your favourite title. A very amusing site, admittedly more for women, but men should see the funny side even if they do feel they are being picked on a little bit.

http://www.grownmencry.com/hhh/STP.html

★ ★

:: BITCH LETTER

Women around the world will be pleased to know that, somewhere out there, there is a funny man named

Mark who has created one of the most exciting, rewarding, fulfilling ways for us to rant like never before. I introduce you to the Bitch Letter Generator. Here you'll have fun generating your own individualised hate letter by choosing words and phrases from a dropdown box and, once it's completed, you can send your bitch letter off to whoever has done you wrong and revel at your bitchy achievement. But, guys, fear not: you have your chance to put it all right again with Mark's equally fitting Apology Note Generator. Suckers!

http://www.karmafarm.com/letter.html

★ ★

:: MARRY AN UGLY MILLIONAIRE

Are you an exceedingly attractive single person looking to pursue your chosen career but can't seem to get that lucky break or indeed be able to fund the lifestyle you deserve? Do you long for someone to hang on to your every word, worship the ground you walk on and smother you with designer clothes, expensive cars and glittering jewels? If you answered yes to all of the above, this next website is going to be your ticket out of Pound Stretcher and straight into Gucci. Marry an Ugly Millionaire is one of the most successful online dating sites due to its win–win attitude. Ugly millionaires can find themselves a beautiful partner, and attractive, money-hungry, poor people can live the life they've always dreamed of. One of the shallowest sites around, but it actually makes people happy.

http://www.marry-an-ugly-millionaire-online-dating-agency.com

★ ★

:: MASTURBATE FOR PEACE

What better way to put an end to war and hatred than by loving one another? But in order to love your neighbour you must love yourself first. This website, which advocates this notion by promoting self-satisfaction, invites citizens to masturbate for peace and to sign their petition to become one of more than 17,000 people worldwide to join the movement. The site also supplies you with information on how to get the best out of your personal pleasure in the form of medication, toys and real-life stories to aid you in your quest for self-love. Show your support to the cause by sporting a bumper sticker to let people know that you're doing your bit for world peace!

http://www.masturbateforpeace.com

★ ★

:: MILKMEN

Many women around the world are keen to breastfeed their infants for reasons of nutrition and love, but often feel that being constantly tied to their baby after carrying them around for nine months can be quite demanding mentally and physically. With the idea that their spouses can take over the role of breastfeeding their offspring, women are fast becoming more than happy to allow this seemingly unnatural process to take place. Men often feel left out of the bonding process, so what better way for them to be more physically involved than nursing their own child? This website aims to educate couples on how to achieve male lactation and act as a support network for parents around the world. Seriously, check it out!

http://www.unassistedchildbirth.com/miscarticles/milkm en.html

★ ★

:: PUSSY PUCKER POTS

These sweetly scented lip balms are the brainchild of lesbian and feminist Stacy Bias, who aims to promote progressive feminist principles of sex and body positivity through the enjoyment of these tasty treats. With a variety of no fewer than 12 frivolous flavours to choose from, such as Chocolate Nipple Ripple and

Strawberry Snatch, these mouth-watering lip balms, intended for lips north of the hips, are a novel way not only to take care of your pout, but to have a little fun with too. Using only natural ingredients means that it is 100 per cent safe for vegans to use, which is a bonus for all those non-meat-eating women among you.

http://www.pussypuckerpots.com

★ ★

∷ REAL DOLL

This website is host to the number-one love doll on the market and to some buyers these silicone beauties are lifelong companions. For a hefty price, these remarkably lifelike creations can be tailor-made to suit your requirements, even down to eye colour and breast size. They're made primarily from silicone, and the creative team at Realdoll use technology from Hollywood's top special-effects suppliers to produce the most realistic love dolls in the world. With Realdoll ever expanding their products, you are now able to buy a male version of the doll, and they have also talked about creating a 'she-male' or hermaphrodite doll, bringing a whole new dimension to the world of sex to suit every desire.

http://www.realdoll.com

★ ★

:: SCREAMING QUEENS

These guys at Screaming Queens definitely know how to throw a good party. Founded by Alex Heimberg, more commonly known to New York's downtown glitterati as 'Miss Understood', he had the aim of bringing his experiences of the flamboyant underworld drag scene on to the party dance floor. With a plethora of singers, impersonators, tribute acts and dancers, there is something to suit every taste and budget. My personal favourites are the strolling human dessert tables in the style of Marie Antoinette, where the food literally comes to its guests in the most dramatic ways, darling!

http://www.screamingqueens.com

★ ★

:: STEEL GIRL

This website is home to female artists worldwide who create their work through the medium of steel. It's a feminist site promoting the works of women who are flourishing in a seemingly male-dominated profession, and gives insights into their artistic interests. Purchase some of the works on this site, be it jewellery or clothing, or enter yourself into current competitions that aim to promote art and anti-government mind-reading technology. Just don't mess with these girls – their first love is metal, and they're not afraid to use it!

http://www.steelgirl.com

★ ★

:: THE GUYCARD SITE

All you testosterone-charged males out there who take pride in things like drinking beer, fishing and knocking up some dry wall (I never did understand what that last one was) are not complete without your GUYcard. This is your exclusive ID to prove to the world that you are one of many men who are proud to be of the male species, and know what it's like to live up to your manly duties. Before obtaining your GUYcard, you must first take the Guy Test in order to officially become a member of this elite club. Should you fail the test, you will still be eligible for a 'Girlie Man Card', but not for the official GUYcard itself. Good luck, and, most of all, be strong like the man that you are. Grrrr!

http://www.guycard.com

★ ★

:: WORLDWIDE WANK

This website aims to rid the world of the taboo subject of masturbation. With statistics showing that 98 per cent of people in the US alone have admittedly carried out the act at least once in their lives, it's a wonder why the remaining 2 per cent aren't looked upon as being the ones with the problem. This website also hosts the world's largest collection of masturbation synonyms. With more than 150,000 different phrases relating to both sexes, you could spend all day here choosing your favourite term. An eye-opening site into a topic not usually discussed so openly, but, with their in-your-face approach to the subject, you'll soon feel right at home.

http://www.worldwidewank.com

★ ★

:: HOME DAD

Are you a stay-at-home dad who does all the cooking and cleaning and cares for the kids while your spouse is out at work? Or maybe you are a single father bringing up your kids alone. Well, this website is an online community for men just like you, and the site is there to offer help, support and advice. It's run by a team of stay-at-home dads who understand the demands of having to juggle work with bringing up children. Wouldn't they save themselves a lot of time and effort by getting a woman to advise them on the topic? After all, they are the experts!

http://www.homedad.org.uk

★ ★

:: MAIL—ORDER HUSBANDS

Ladies, it's your turn to take your pick of all those single men on the market looking for their future bride. Take the online compatibility test to find out who your best suitor would be, then sign up to start your bidding. You are also asked to invite all your other single friends along to join in with the action. Now play fair — it's only right that you share your knowledge. Isn't that what friends are for?

http://www.mailorderhusbands.net

★ ★

:: LOVE NOTES

This website is brought to you by the makers of Durex condoms, promoting safe sex as well as spreading a little love to your partner in the form of a naughty e-card. A fun interactive site where you can choose from a range of different personalities, backgrounds and message content to send off to your unsuspecting lover. Imagine your partner's face when this saucy email from you pops up in their inbox. You'll definitely be in their good books, so best cancel your plans for that evening as you may be in for a reciprocated treat!

http://www.durexsex.com

★ ★

SOCIETY AND CULTURE

THIS CHAPTER DEPICTS how diverse we are as human beings, not just culturally but socially. As you plunge into the depths of people's likes and dislikes, phobias and obsessions, you will bear witness to the outrageous world of what makes us humans tick. Find out what we like to collect, societies we belong to and things that really get under our skin, but most importantly keep an open mind and try not to get too sucked in!

:: THE TOILET MUSEUM

Join the sanitation crusade. This website is dedicated to the evolution of disposal of human waste, seen as a critical part of the development of human civilisation. Crammed with education about the history of the bog, as well as elaborate pictures of piss pots throughout the ages, it takes you on a virtual tour of this India-based museum, where never before has the toilet been treated with such importance. If you thought it all started with an invention by an Englishman called Thomas Crapper, you'd be wrong! For an equally good but slightly different version of the Toilet Museum visit http://www.toiletmuseum.com.

http://www.sulabhtoiletmuseum.org

★ ★

:: ELEVATOR RULES

Is there a right or wrong way to stand in a lift? Is there a code of conduct about what people can and can't do or say while travelling between floors in a hotel or an office building? This site says there is and gives an abundant list of dos and don'ts that will provide all involved with a pleasant and correct transporting experience. Read through the anal advice on the codes of conduct that for those who haven't been following them are blamed for the creation of this site. You'll be taught how to press the buttons correctly, how to wait, how to enter, what to do once in motion and how to leave – all of which amounts to the latest important science of elevator etiquette. I guess this means my days of the 'fart and run' game are well and truly over, then.

http://www.elevatorrules.com

★ ★

:: THE DARWIN AWARDS

The essential qualification for inclusion on this site is that you have to be dead. The Darwin Awards make examples of the late great people that once graced this Earth by exhibiting their achievements in the form of an incredible collection of the most absurd and unfortunate experiments and events in history that all went horribly wrong at the hands of these men. The idea is that in order to evolve into a harmonious nation we must encounter these downfalls, learn from our mistakes and pass on this knowledge to future generations. Put bluntly, you do something stupid enough to kill you and are thus removed from the gene pool. Pure Darwinism. Read through examples of this in the form of 'Wife Tossing', 'The Last Supper', 'Lobster Vasectomies' and 'The Scrotum Self Repair Experiment'.

http://www.darwinawards.com

★ ★

:: DULL MEN'S CLUB

Need a good cheering up? Then don't come here. This website was devised for dull men around the world to congregate and share uninteresting tales of life that cool trendy guys would find insignificant. Read through the forum of boring guys talking about things that interest them and follow some of their links to experience their interests. I'm just happy that this group of men have somewhere they feel appreciated and respected, so we should all learn from this site and take the time to turn to the dull guy in the corner of the office, or email the school geek and give them the time of day – if you can tear yourself away from the screen, that is.

http://www.dullmen.com

★ ★

:: TRAFFIC CONES

This is the official website for the Traffic Cone Preservation Society dedicated to all those helpful cones that often get overlooked by motorists and pedestrians alike. A bizarre little site that details all types of cones in various sizes, colours and functions as well as the evolution of the cone and novel toys, games and memorabilia that can be purchased directly from the site. So, the next time you pass a traffic cone in the street, you'll think twice and maybe give it a little smile rather than catching it with your tyres as you zoom past.

http://www.trafficcone.com

★ ★

:: ETIQUETTE HELL

Are you constantly embarrassed by your friends and dread family get-togethers for fear that it will end up in fisticuffs? Well, direct them all to this site for an eye-opening insight on how *not* to behave. Etiquette Hell aspires to teach unruly yobs a thing or two about the correct way to conduct oneself in public. With more than four thousand stories submitted by site visitors, they aim to make examples of these people by teaching them where they went wrong and how to behave in a proper manner. Sod this – I'm off to the pub to create a cracking story to submit to this site.

http://www.etiquettehell.com/content/eh_main/gen/eh_index.shtml

★ ★

:: GOTHIC WEDDINGS

Are you and your partner about to step up your relationship a notch by getting married, but the last thing you envisage your big day to be is traditional and predictable? Well, this site should meet all your needs and enable you to enjoy your unique day with the people you love. Gothic Weddings are fast becoming the choice of theme as many are turning their backs on the traditional white wedding for something more outrageous and extravagant. You don't have to be a goth, vampire or Satan worshipper, tempting as they may sound: you just have to have a little imagination and the desire to be different to ensure you get the dream day you've always desired.

http://www.gothicweddings.com

★ ★

:: HEAD OVER HEELS

Women, brace yourselves, you are about to embark on an experience that may blow your mind. Yes, it's the Museum of Shoes and it is good! This website takes you through a time warp of fashion from prehistoric times right the way through to the ever-so-chic 1980s. Witness how the shoe evolved from a form of protection to a fashion item through a range of archive pictures and narration. Browse through a choice of eras or styles and be sure to check out the funky-shoes section for an alternative selection.

http://www.headoverheelshistory.com

★ ★

:: I HATE CLOWNS

Are you one of the millions of people who suffer from the common phobia of clowns, or, to use its correct term, coulrophobia? If so, then you should find some solace in this site dedicated to the disliking of the annoyingly happy entertainers who have a seemingly sinister side. The site host, Rodney Blackwell, claims not to have a fear of clowns but an extreme dislike of them, and uses this site to vent his pet hate. It is now in its tenth year of campaigning against clowns, and you are invited to share your stories with the world and explain exactly what it is that gets you all hot under the collar when it comes to these circus freaks.

http://www.ihateclowns.com

★ ★

:: STRANGE VEHICLES

The title of this site is pretty self-explanatory, as you are faced with all the weirdest vehicles the site creators could find. Included in this site are lists of strange pages featuring strange photos, strange news and strange humour as well as the 28 International Rules of Manhood. Start from the top and work your way down, as you wouldn't want to miss out on any of this madness. And if, by chance, you feel they haven't included a very important strange element that you know about, send in your ideas along with any pictures and add them to the collection of oddball entries.

http://www.strangevehicles.com

★ ★

:: CREATIVE FOOTBALL COOKIE

This website points the finger at society in such a way that it aims to wipe out all the people in it who just aren't pulling their weight. It highlights the inadequacies of certain groups of people, making a spectacle of them for the betterment of the human race. On this site expect to find a direct, harsh and unforgiving approach to saying what is really on people's minds in the form of short stories and essays depicting the bad and the worse. The site may come across as being super-negative but the underlying point is one of a more positive nature and really these guys are nothing more than a vocal bunch of confused pussycats.

http://www.mindspring.com/~bft23

★ ★

:: INTERNATIONAL BUSINESS CARD COLLECTORS

For those of you who are into collecting business cards – and I bet there are many of you – this little site is your online guide to achieving the maximum potential from your hobby. Start off by reading the welcoming introduction, where you'll be met by some friendly text, making you feel part of a unique group. Next, get some expert advice on where the best places are to find cards and also some helpful hints on how to bag the ultimate treasure – a celebrity's business card. Browse through the online library of cards and meet other members like yourself before signing up to become part of a growing society of card-collecting enthusiasts. You won't be sorry you visited this exhilarating site!

http://www.ibccsite.com

★ ★

:: METASPY

Have you ever wondered what the rest of the world is searching for on the Internet? Or do you think you're the only one who has a vivid imagination when it comes to locating obscure sites for your personal pleasure? This website is the creator of MetaCrawler, a unique program that claims it can search the Net to see what other users are trying to locate. So you fancy yourself as a bit of a voyeur, do you? Then this site should reassure you that you're just as odd as the rest of them. Slightly creepy but extremely entertaining as you delve into an unknown world of people's deepest darkest desires – either that or you'll just witness the usual day-to-day searches of normal people, in which case it can be pretty boring.

http://www.metaspy.com

★ ★

:: INTERNATIONAL PAPERWEIGHT SOCIETY

Without seeming to be rude, this is possibly the most boring site that you will visit throughout this entire book, unless of course you are an avid paperweight enthusiast. If you are, I apologise if you find my words insulting. OK, so paperweights are hardly exciting, but you would have thought that the site creators could have jazzed the page up a bit with some eye-catching colours, or elaborated on the text making the content more appealing to strangers to the world of paperweights. My advice to you is to move on quickly before you find yourself signing up for the newsletter and subjecting yourself to more painstaking torture of the paperweight kind.

http://mall.turnpike.net/~ips/ips.html

★ ★

:: UGLIEST CARS IN BRITAIN

To me, a car is a car, but apparently vanity spreads across to transport and nowhere is more tuned into this subject than this website. These shallow people have segregated all the ugly cars throughout the years and displayed them on this site for all to leer at. They would rather overlook the fact that these so-called ugly cars have been responsible for getting their owners from A to B and back again, and judge them on appearance alone. Shallow, I hear you cry? It's downright heartbreaking!

http://www.uglycars.co.uk

★ ★

:: POST SECRET

Do you have hidden desires that are bursting to get out? Or maybe you are harbouring secrets from your past that are eating you up inside. If so, this website might be just the release you need. It's in the form of a blog, where you are invited to send in your secrets anonymously. Get as creative and artistic as you like, whether your message is apparent or obscure. The only requirement is that you create your secrets on a standard-sized postcard, and the rest is up to you.

http://postsecret.blogspot.com

★ ★

:: SINKIES

Are you so busy that the thought of preparing a meal, let alone eating it and clearing up, is enough to bring on a minor panic attack? Well, don't worry, you are not alone. There are many people across the world who share the same phobia of taking time out of their busy schedule to sit down and eat a proper meal. These people are known as sinkies, and they actually live normal happy lives due to the practical way they approach meal times. Forget all the preparation, taking time to eat slowly, and finally the mundane task of clearing up – just eat from the fridge or over the sink and cut your meal times in half but still manage to get the job done. This site will revolutionise the way you eat food for ever – and to think they've been doing this for 16 years now, that's some achievement!

http://www.sinkie.com

★ ★

:: THE VIRTUAL CORKSCREW MUSEUM

If you thought corkscrews were of interest only to those who drink wine, this site will show you otherwise. The creators have dedicated it to their beloved collection of corkscrews and it's a place where like-minded people with the same passions can congregate and discuss topics of the screwing nature. With 30 rooms brimming with as much metal as you could wish to see, you'll be hard pushed to find a collection like this anywhere else.

http://www.bullworks.net/virtual.htm

★ ★

:: THE HUMAN VIRUS SCANNER

Have you ever wondered if our brains are infected with viruses, just like computers? This website aims to put across this argument by inviting its visitors to use their online human virus scanner. Getting scanned couldn't be easier: you just highlight the images that are familiar to you and wait for the end result of how many viruses you contain. You'll be surprised at just how polluted your mind is with everyday advertisements warping your mind. But don't worry too much as they have practical, if a little harsh, clean-up advice that will rid your head of such controlling thoughts.

http://totl.net/VirusScanner

★ ★

:: WHAT THE HECK!

One man's trash is another man's treasure and never has this saying been truer than on this website. The site creators spend their days trawling the Net looking for items that people are selling and feature them on their site. Sounds pretty normal so far, but if you look closer at the items you will see that they are not the sort of everyday thing that most people would consider to be a real find. An 11-inch white penis, 24 children, and the nails from a serial killer are all up for grabs. While some are more politically correct than others, you'll be stunned and amused at the diverse range of things that people will sell.

http://www.whattheheck.com

★ ★

:: TECH TALES

This hilarious site pokes fun at computer-illiterate people by highlighting their stupidities for all to see. Browse through the archives of absurd re-enactments dating back to 1997, where conversations between tech-support workers and their clueless customers have been scripted out. I recommend you choose the option of listening to the conversations first to get the most out of this site. If you are a troubled tech-support worker and deal with clueless people like this on a daily basis, you are invited to send in your experiences to the site to be added to the ever-growing collection. A must for computer boffins, tech supporters or those who understand that their desktop isn't something your computer rests on.

http://www.techtales.com

★ ★

:: WEIRD

Due to the nature of this book and of course its title, I decided to see what would come up if I typed 'www.weird.com' into the address bar. What I expected to find was a wacky off-the-wall site containing all the oddness of the Net, but instead some clever people have bought the domain name and used it for – well, pretty much nothing. Proving that, in the fast-paced world of the Internet, good website names are hard to come by so get 'em while you can. That said, though, there is some content on the site that could be of interest, but my guess is you would have to be severely bored or actually know the site creators to get any enjoyment out of it at all. So here it is, the not-so-weird weird.com.

http://www.weird.com

★ ★

:: BREAK THE CHAIN

One thing that email users worldwide can unanimously say is that we hate junk mail and those annoying spam emails. This informative site aims to open our eyes to the evil world of poisonous mail, preventing us from going mad when trying to claw through our inbox on a Monday morning, or, worse, having our identity nicked. Read through some of the most common and current email hoaxes and urban legends circulating the Net and educate yourself on how to keep up your guard against the terror mail. Join the fight against junk mail by submitting any spam you may have received to warn others of its presence. Together we can put an end to inbox spamming!

http://breakthechain.org

★ ★

:: FOREST

This is the website of the pro-smoking group FOREST, which stands for the Freedom Organisation for the Right to Enjoy Smoking Tobacco. Yes, you heard me correctly: these guys are famous for controversially supporting the rights of smokers worldwide and say bollocks to anyone who tells them otherwise. It was founded in 1979 by a former Battle of Britain fighter pilot and pipe smoker who got the right royal hump when puffing on his pipe while waiting for a train, when an old dear demanded he put his smoking apparatus out. He was so outraged that he rounded up a few of his smoking cronies and FOREST was founded on this basis. Follow the organisation's many campaigns and, if you feel the urge, get involved – I'm sure you'll be more than welcome in the fight against the national smoking ban. Good luck with that one, FOREST!

http://www.forestonline.org

★ ★

SCIENCE AND NATURE

THE INTERNET HAS fast become a place for information sources, and what better way to keep in touch with the latest scientific developments than through the accessible use of the Web? The main problem encountered with this freedom to display one's discoveries is the diversity of content exhibited for all to see, and, as a viewer browsing these pages, one can find it difficult to tell the difference between breakthrough findings and Internet hoaxes. Within this chapter, you will witness the groundbreaking, exciting, unusual and just plain idiotic theories of many a mad scientist. Expect to learn a lot and remember always to keep an open mind – after all, you can't believe everything you read!

:: MOON CITIZENSHIP

Want to become an official citizen of the moon? This website will tell you how. This is the official website of the Lunar Republic Society. The site features all the latest news on planned moon landings as well as the low-down on settlement, tourism, resources, a crater catalogue, plus a dictionary of moon vocabulary to keep you up to date with all the latest lingo. View the *Full Moon Atlas* for a detailed guide to the satellite and take a sneak peek at your next possible holiday destination – a must for genuine lunatics!

http://www.lunarrepublic.com

★ ★

:: SAND FACTS

Ever thought sand was the most interesting substance in the universe? Well, you're in good company: this is a site put together by the International Society Dedicated to the Interests of Sand Collectors. Learn the basics of what sand is and how to become a collector – presumably, it takes more than just a trip down to the beach. Get educated on how always to be prepared in the event that you come across an interesting sand sample by receiving one of their sand-discovery kits, and be sure to sign up for free membership to be the first to hear about all your sand news and gossip.

http://www.sandcollectors.org

★ ★

:: WACKY USES

This website was created by eccentric scientist Joey Green. His mission is to turn around the way in which we look at everyday household objects and realise that they are not fulfilling their full potential. Take your pick from coffee, peanut butter, toothpicks, tennis balls, honey, nail polish, salad dressing, paper towels, baby wipes, clingfilm, chalk, toothpaste and hair conditioner, and discover the many different uses these household items can be applied to. Learn how to use these items to conduct experiments around the home as well as discovering weird unknown facts about the products you are purchasing.

http://www.wackyuses.com

★ ★

:: DATA DESTRUCTION

Ever wondered what to do with all the excess CDs lying around in your house that you will never use again? Yes, you could just throw them out in the good old-fashioned way, but this website urges you to have a little fun with them before deciding on their final resting place. CD nuking is the latest craze sweeping the nation providing pyrotechnics and computer geeks alike with an experimental hobby that will produce different results every time. Follow the online time guide, which will tell you how long you should microwave your CD to gain the desired effect, and then marvel at your work of art while resuscitating your cat from the poisonous fumes! This website comes with a caution and should not be viewed without the supervision of a responsible adult.

http://toast.ardant.net

★ ★

:: WORLD'S TALLEST MAN

This website is home to Robert Pershing Wadlow, who is recorded as being the tallest man in medical history. Wadlow was born in 1918 in Illinois, weighing in at 8.7 pounds, but from then on he shot up like a rocket and didn't stop growing until he reached a soaring 8 foot 11.1 inches. His giant-like appearance was due to an overactive pituitary gland, which was discovered just before his 12th birthday, when he was already well over 6 foot 5 inches. Read about his amazing life and view the online album of photos depicting the man who was known as the Gentle Giant.

http://www.altonweb.com/history/wadlow

★ ★

:: ASK DR SCIENCE

Are you bursting with unanswered questions about scientific mysteries that have been troubling you for years? Well, fret no more, because Dr Science is here to answer all your questions. And with a degree in the subject he is more than qualified to lend a hand. Americans can catch Dr Science on several radio shows, where he gives out free advice to troubled listeners. Something of an enigma himself, he is rarely seen out and prefers the privacy of his own domain, but is always willing to help people out of their misery online. Go ahead, try him.

http://www.drscience.com

★ ★

:: TO INFINITY AND BEYOND!

This fascinating website has been documenting pictures of our universe every day since 16 June 1995. With lots to be learned and amazing sights to be seen, this website challenges all others when it comes to consistency, and you'll be hard pushed to find another site that will give you as many different types of search options as this one. View a backdated library of images, each accompanied by a brief explanation written by a professional astronomer, or so they will have us believe – you can't be too careful who you trust on the Internet nowadays.

http://antwrp.gsfc.nasa.gov/apod/archivepix.html

★ ★

:: BRITISH BEEKEEPERS ASSOCIATION

This is home to the British Beekeepers Association or the BBKA. Here beekeepers and enthusiasts from around the world can congregate in one place to obsess about those honey-loving insects that you either love or hate. Visit this site and become a member. Book a course or even a holiday as well as receiving help and advice on what to do if you are faced with a nest or a swarm of bees. An interesting site if you are curious about the life of the honeybee; otherwise a complete washout. But at least you'll know what to do in the event of a bee attack.

http://www.bbka.org.uk

★ ★

:: LIFE EXTENSION FOUNDATION

So you like the idea of living for ever, to outgrow your peers and watch as the world evolves around you? How about being cryonically frozen to wake up in a future time and feel as if you'd just been in a deep sleep? This website aims to show you how. The Alcor Life Extension Foundation is the world leader in cryonics, cryonics research and cryonics technology. Its groundbreaking team of staff, with cutting-edge technology, feel that the ability to preserve human life, resulting in life extension, is not a far-off goal. You are invited to become a member of the foundation by filling out a membership form and following the detailed payment plan that the website states as being 'surprisingly affordable'. Make your own mind up on that one!

http://www.alcor.org

★ ★

:: EARTH'S MYSTERIES

Many theories behind some of Earth's mysteries are not always taken seriously by modern-day scientists, since these explanations are too far-fetched to be labelled scientific. The study of Earth's mysteries is now considered a multi-disciplined or holistic approach towards ancient sites and landscapes, and is generally regarded with suspicion by academics. Explore this site on its journey through the unexplained mysteries of the natural world and draw your own conclusions as to their validity or otherwise.

http://witcombe.sbc.edu/earthmysteries

★ ★

:: FLY POWER

If you think that the fly is more than just a disease-spreading nuisance and wish to put its functions to a more practical positive use, then you've stumbled across the exact site for your needs. Purchase the FlyPower Model Aeroplane Kit, which includes all the material you will need to construct two fully functional aeroplanes utilising a common housefly as the engine. If you can get past the annoyingly persistent fly that follows you around the page, it's a very interesting and eye-opening site that is well worth a visit for a chuckle if nothing else.

http://www.flypower.com

★ ★

:: THE ARTICULATION PAGE

Does the idea of constructing your own skeleton from scratch get you all of a flutter with excitement and joy?

If so, this is the site for you. Visit this site to make your dream come true in this how-to guide for even the simplest of minds. Find out why people just like you love this site as it aids them in their quest and read their real-life success stories. Follow the online steps from gathering supplies to the end result – your completed articulated skeleton. And if you get stuck you can always refer back to the skeleton enthusiasts' favourite old spiritual, 'Dem Bones'. Now hear the word of the Lord!

http://www-adm.pdx.edu/user/bio/articula/home.html

★ ★

THE TENTH DIMENSION

Brace yourselves for probably the biggest mind-bender of your lives with this website detailing the scientific explanation of the tenth dimension. Now I won't ruin your experience by explaining what it's about. I'll just leave it to your discretion to figure out the true meaning, as I did when I first visited the site. I will, however, challenge anybody not to get completely and utterly lost and confused to the point that they'll be ripping their hair out with frustration.

http://www.tenthdimension.com/flash2.php

★ ★

:: ALEX CHIU

This is the website of controversial wacky scientist Alex Chiu, who claims he has invented a device to reverse the ageing process and even lead to physical immortality if worn on a daily basis. Read his scientific explanation, which has baffled sceptics around the world, and find out about other products that, it is claimed, will have you outliving your great-grandchildren in an ever-youthful and illness-free manner. Banned by Google (although a search will bring up several sites that *refer* to Chiu), this site is well worth visiting, if only to see what all the fuss is about.

http://www.alexchiu.com

★ ★

:: SILLY-NAMED MOLECULES

This website will prove that science doesn't need to be boring and can in fact be fun. Join the rest of the so-called geeks around the world and revel in the jovial game of finding molecules with silly names. Browse through a mammoth library of humorously named molecules, each with an explanation and corresponding picture or diagram. You haven't lived until you've visited this site!

http://www.chm.bris.ac.uk/sillymolecules/sillymols.html

★ ★

:: ANIMALS IN THE WOMB

This is the website of the National Geographic Channel and host to the groundbreaking programme *Animals in the Womb*. View the online trailer of the programme to discover the advance technology that is able to capture these animals in four-dimensional forms before they are even born and get an insight into the unique developments of these creatures. Also featured on this site are behind-the-scenes facts about how it was filmed as well as the detailed synopsis on the subject of animal pregnancy. A great site where animal enthusiasts, scientists and anyone with an interest in evolution can come and be amazed at the imagery and facts in store.

http://www9.nationalgeographic.com/channel/inthewomb animals

★ ★

:: RON'S ANGELS

Are you set on having the perfect-looking child with a beautiful appearance that will provide them with a head start in life? Well, let me introduce you to Ron Harris. Ron has carefully handpicked gorgeous males and females who have gone through a gruelling application process to be among the many 'perfect' people who qualify to be sperm and egg donors. So, if you only want the best of offspring to continue your legacy of good looks and popularity, sign up for membership and browse through all of the beauty, and if someone takes your fancy you can bid online to secure your ideal donor. Shallow? Never – it's the ultimate gift to your unborn child.

http://www.ronsangels.com/index2.html

★ ★

:: THE 28–HOUR DAY

This website is for everyone who feels there are not enough hours in the day, days in the week, weeks in the month, etc., etc. Do you wake up in the morning feeling as if you'd only just gone to sleep, or maybe when it's bedtime the last thing you want to do is sleep and would much rather do something more mentally or physically stimulating? Cheeky! Well, this site proposes the 28-hour day, whereby the week would be shorter by a day, but we will have gained four hours on our day. Trust me, it makes sense – just look at the site.

http://dbeat.com/28

★ ★

:: THE MYSTERY SPOT

The Mystery Spot is an area about 150 feet in diameter located in the redwood forests just outside of Santa Cruz, California. This place is unlike any other found on Earth, as the area is claimed to defy the laws of gravity and physics to the extent that people have been witnessed walking up walls and performing acts that would be impossible in any normal environment. Read up on the history of the Mystery Spot since its discovery in 1939 and even book your tickets online to visit the much-talked-about location. Witness the pictures of past visitors and their experiences of the Mystery Spot. And, to give you another idea about this crazy place, remember the Lionel Richie video for the 1980s classic 'Dancing on the Ceiling'? It was shot there – really it was!

http://www.mysteryspot.com

★ ★

:: VHEMT

We as humans find it most natural to reproduce and create a family who will follow our legacy long after we are dead and buried, and we don't really think of the consequences of what reproduction has on the world. This website – created by its founder, Les U Knight – aims to promote human extinction, allowing the Earth to be restored to its former glory, leaving the natural elements to evolve and die out without the human race intervening. Read through this lengthy informative site and see if you are willing to join the Voluntary Human Extinction Movement, whose motto is 'May we live long and die out'.

http://www.vhemt.org

★ ★

SPORT AND RECREATION

THROUGHOUT THIS CHAPTER, you will get an insight into the many different worlds of sport and recreation, ranging from the extremely dangerous to the mind-numbingly boring. It's hard to believe that these activities have such huge followings and even more surprising that they have carried on for as long as they have. But what they all have in common are dedicated members who make their chosen pastime not just an activity but a way of life. Prepare yourself as you embark on some of the weirdest activities out there today and realise that, when it comes to sport and recreation, there really are no limits.

:: ROMANIAN MINT RUBBING

Traditionally, mint-rubbing customs have been kept within national borders, passed from generation to generation by word of mouth. But now, with the power of technology, these remarkable skills are out there for the whole world to learn about and can be found on this site. And, as if pure and simple mint rubbing were not enough, there's also information about advanced techniques involving cats' tails, leaves and dogs together with esoteric research into rain, manganese rubbing and lying with your belly facing the sun. Baffled? Me too.

http://www.mintrubbing.org

★ ★

:: EXTREME IRONING

Who said ironing was just for housewives and the hired help? This site will propel you into the world of ironing like you've never seen before, turning up the heat on a new craze that is sweeping the nation. On this site, you will be introduced to the many ways of using the old elbow grease in the form of ironing under water, in the Artic Circle and as part of a sky-diving exercise. Find out about how one enthusiast took extreme ironing to a nudist beach and how the sport has become so popular in Taiwan that it has been made into a regular drama on Public Service Television. Push yourself to the limits with this site, putting the days of mundane ironing in your kitchen firmly in the past.

http://www.extremeironing.com

★ ★

:: WHISTLING

Are you constantly being told to shut up when you're sitting at your desk at work and whistling a happy tune? This site celebrates people like you who want to put whistling on the map as an underrated exercise that often goes unnoticed. This site has everything you need if you want to become a virtuoso whistler. The only one of its kind in cyberspace, there are hundreds of downloads featuring natural whistlers like parakeets and canaries, and famous whistlers past and present who turn classical and popular musicals into wind-blowing masterpieces. Ideal if you want to work up a party piece for a special occasion, or to perfect your skill of pissing off the boss.

http://www.whistlingrecords.com

★ ★

:: THE GOLF BALL LIBERATION ARMY

Golf balls may seem to you like insignificant objects that are thrashed around the golf course for your pleasure and recreation, but this site is the voice of these poor little mites and highlights the real horror stories that these tiny balls encounter on a daily basis. Browse through the pages of terrible tales including the horror of the gold ball washer, why Tiger Woods is the Antichrist and how you can get involved in putting a stop to cruelty to golf balls worldwide. This eye-opening site will liberate golf balls everywhere and reveal the truth behind the seemingly harmless sport.

http://www.freewebs.com/golfballarmy

★ ★

:: LAWNMOWER RACING

This is the official website of the British Lawnmower Racing Association with all the information you could possibly want about how it works, race results, a racing calendar and how to become a member. Read up on the history of the association and watch the thrilling video to give you a greater insight into the sport. Join other grass cutters by jumping on your trusted mower and, instead of using it to cut the lawn, convert it into a mean machine to race against other blade runners from around the country.

http://www.blmra.co.uk

★ ★

:: BED MATTRESS SPOTTING

Never mind trainspotting. This site from Belgium captures the latest craze in spotting bed mattresses that have been dumped in obscure places. There are hundreds of pictorial submissions detailing locations and dates from all over the world with the majority, interestingly, coming from Britain. Never again will you be able to walk past a crusty old mattress and complain about the state of our streets – make like the homeless and get excited!

http://www.streetmattress.com

★ ★

:: DRAIN SPOTTING

This website welcomes you into the world of drain spotting, where you'll learn the history of drain covers and the artistic elements in how they were designed. If you were expecting a detailed analysis on the function of drains, then you've come to the wrong place: this site is all about face value and isn't interested in the depths underneath the surface. The site creators urge you to look down and take note the next time you walk over a drain and admire its design and creativity rather than simply stroll past it, ignoring its existence, as most inconsiderate people with somewhere to go do.

http://www.drainspotting.com

★ ★

:: EXTREME CHICK FIGHTS

If you thought fighting was just for guys you are sorely mistaken. Visit this website for an uncensored insight into the world of chick fighting, where only the nastiest girls win. Follow your favourite fighter and get all the info on up and coming fights, or watch video clips of these women in action, pissed off and fully charged to kick some arse and take names. Sugar and spice and all things nice? Definitely not what *these* girls are made of.

http://www.chickfight.tv

★ ★

:: OKIE NOODLING

So you may have heard of this sport before, but if like me you are a virgin to the world of noodling you may be shocked at what you're about to see. This pastime is usually reserved for programmes on the Discovery Channel, and this site is home to the feature-length documentary *Okie Noodling*, which depicts the sport at first hand. Noodling is the age-old sport of catching 50–60-pound catfish with your bare hands. Banned in some states of America, the seemingly dangerous sport has a cult following due to its risk element, and has become so popular it has been turned into a competition. Definitely not for beginners or those with a dislike of water – or of big fish with big teeth.

http://www.okienoodling.com

★ ★

:: RIDE ACCIDENTS

This site will put you off theme-park rides for life as it depicts the worst accidents from around the world. Get up-to-the-minute news on all the latest attractions, finding out what not to go on, and follow updates on when rides that have been closed down will reopen. Read through hundreds of fairground horror stories that turned a fun day out into a ride from hell. Personally, I've never trusted anything that can fold up on to the back of a lorry and be hurtled down the M1 at 70 mph, then erected in a flooded field only to throw you into the air and spin you round a million times. Two words: barking mad!

http://www.rideaccidents.com

★ ★

:: STRANGE BUT TRUE

This website has the answers to all the unusual and obscure questions that have been buzzing around your head all those years. So strange, in fact, that these questions may have never crossed your mind before, but with an archive full of interesting facts you can impress your friends with your pointless but informative knowledge and hope that at least one of them comes up in your next pub quiz.

http://sbt.bhmedia.com

★ ★

:: UGLY FOOTBALLERS

Soccer stars are usually renowned for their good looks and toned physiques, leading them to secure sponsorship deals for advertising campaigns. This immediately raises their profile and feeds their bank balance. And of course the picture is not complete without the token WAGs (wives and girlfriends) to spend all their hard-earned cash on designer clothes and interior designs for their newly purchased mansion. Well, this site pays tribute to the not-so-fortunate players who may be just as talented in the playing department but lack the looks that will give them the entire package needed today to become a football media darling. Hold on to your mullets – there are some sights to see here.

http://www.uglyfootballers.com

★ ★

EDUCATION AND RECRUITMENT

THE INTERNET HOLDS a vast source of information for those of you who want to find their chosen professions. It is also an excellent way of researching your prospective line of work and provides a multitude of educational outlets for you to learn about almost anything to do with education and recruitment. Within this chapter, you will get an insight into the world's worst jobs and find out what they entail. You will also get the chance to educate yourself on previously unknown topics to gain a greater knowledge of what kind of wacky jobs there are out there. Check out websites that will help you once you are employed, giving you excuses for lateness, or psychological tests to put you in the right line of business. There is something here for everyone – from ostrich farming to embalming dead bodies – so go on, grab a spoon!

:: SHORTCUT ESSAYS

A must for schoolchildren and college kids with homework essays to write, who want to cut corners and save time. Simply type in your subject and this site will produce all the work for you. Every subject imaginable is covered, from investment banking to Michael Jackson's mothball collection. And no two essays are ever the same, so you can even produce extras and sell them on to your fellow students! All is not what it seems, though, and I think once the essay is marked there will be some students with a valuable lesson learned about cutting corners.

http://www.EssayGenerator.com

★ ★

:: THE WORLD'S WORST JOBS

Thinking about changing your career? Fed up with your boring nine-to-five job? Well, take a look at this site and it will make you think twice about throwing in the towel and will probably make you appreciate your current job all the more. Within this website, you will witness horrendous stories from people who claim to have the worst jobs in the world. From worm taster to barnyard masturbator, the most hellish jobs are listed here. Read about the worst-paid jobs, as well as bosses from hell and CVs that are so bad they make you want to meet the person just to see what they are really like. Burger Bar, I'm coming back – all is forgiven!

http://www.worst-jobs.com

★ ★

:: BRITISH INSTITUTE OF EMBALMERS

Although handling and preparing dead bodies isn't the average person's favourite pastime, these dedicated workers are so serious and passionate about their chosen career they have set up an institute dedicated to the profession. Founded in 1927 by a group of funeral directors, the Institute has as its main purpose to educate and inform people of the science of embalming the dead, thus making it less of a taboo and more of a common occurrence. Read up on the full history of the institute and, if it tickles your fancy, apply for membership and start a whole new career in embalming. One thing's for sure: you'll never be out of work.

http://www.bioe.org.uk

★ ★

:: CUSTOMERS SUCK

If you have the pleasure of dealing with obnoxious customers on a daily basis and feel as if you're all alone in the world dealing with everything from the absurd to the downright rude, fear not. This website is probably the only place where like-minded people can tell their tales of nightmarish customers without the fear of losing their job for telling a customer where to get off. Join in the online forums as a therapeutic way to let off steam from a hard day's work and judge among your peers as to who has had to deal with the worst customer of the day. But, whatever you do, don't complain, or you'll be out on your ear.

http://www.customerssuck.com

★ ★

:: GHETTO KIDS

Do you suspect your children are following a life of crime and gang warfare? Is your four-year-old showing signs of thug mentality among its peers and you're worried it's spiralling out of control? Well, Ghetto Kids Hood is here to help. This website is here to educate children and adults alike on the reality of the world they are growing up in, and how to combat the enemy that is 'peer pressure'. Through the use of the ghetto kids, your children can learn by example what it's like growing up in a tough neighbourhood and how to avoid getting into situations that may turn them into mini-thugs. You can even purchase online the doll that you feel most represents your troubled tot in an attempt to keep them on the straight and narrow.

http://www.ghettokidshood.com/index.html

★ ★

:: MORTUARY SCHOOL

Do you have a burning desire to succeed in life but are still waiting for your calling? Or maybe you are stuck in a boring unchallenging job and are looking for a life-changing career that will be jam-packed with variety and self-fulfilment. Take a look at this site. You may be surprised at what it has to offer. The National Academy of Mortuary Science could be what you are seeking. Everything from hearse driving to becoming a mortuary technician is here, and the academy also gives you the option of studying from home for added flexibility. View the step-by-step guide to how the course will pan out, prepping you up so that there are no scary surprises. It's the perfect career. Just think, you'll be working with people on a daily basis who won't answer you back, will always do as you tell them and will never be able to sue you should the worst happen. Give me corpses over kids any day.

http://www.drkloss.com

★ ★

:: OSTRICH FARMING

Never has your future looked rosier than checking out this website and following its steps to becoming a fully fledged ostrich farmer. Live the lifestyle you always wanted. Say goodbye to the formalities of the corporate world. Never again will you be penalised for going two minutes over your lunch break or be frowned upon for calling your mate during working hours. As an ostrich farmer, you will be your own boss and have free range to work however you like. And, if you happen to be an ostrich enthusiast, you'll have landed yourself a dream job – although, if you're not, by the end of reading through this website, with all this fabulous information on the bird, you might be.

http://www.ostrichresources.com/indexb.php

★ ★

:: GRAVESTONE STUDIES

The Association for Gravestone Studies (AGS) was founded in 1977 for the purpose of studying the preservation and artistic makeup that is connected with these homes for the deceased. Many people overlook the structural content of a gravestone as merely concrete slabs on which we remember loved ones past, but some gravestones have a lot more to them than we would like to credit them for. Read through this site to educate yourself on the history of gravestones and all that is associated with them. A particularly boring site, but someone out there must give a damn, because it is very detailed, to say the least.

http://www.gravestonestudies.org

★ ★

:: TEST YOURSELF

Have you always wondered what kind of person you really are? Are you often told that you're in the wrong line of business and would be much better suited to being a paparazzo than to being a part-time trolley collector at the local supermarket? With so many career paths to choose from and the fast-paced world we live in, we can often overlook our true calling and sell ourselves short by sticking to what we think we know best about ourselves. Now let's face it, there is absolutely nothing wrong with collecting trolleys, but there must come a time when you think to yourself, I wasn't born to do this – I can achieve more. This website provides you with that extra push that you need in the form of online psych tests to determine what type of person you really are and the career path that would best suit you. Now these tests are to be taken at your own risk and I am in no way to be held responsible for their outcome. Just thought I'd clear that up.

http://www.psychtests.com/tests/career/index.html

★ ★

:: JACKPOT!

It's everybody's dream to win the lottery, and, even though it would be a life-changing experience, most people don't think about the consequences of what money can bring. This website is here to prepare you for that lifestyle change, to protect you from any nasty bumps on your way to becoming mega-rich. Learn about the 'small print' that most people choose to ignore when participating in the lottery, and find out about how you receive your money and, most importantly, how much of it you receive over a period of time. A very interesting site, which will prepare you for the realities of what it's really like to be a lottery winner. Remember, if it sounds too good to be true, it probably is.

http://www.note.com/note/pp/jackpot.html

★ ★

:: USELESS INFORMATION

This website is the brainchild of US science teacher Steve Silverman. His aim with this site is to educate people with stories that, if they hadn't heard them, wouldn't really affect their lives. However, they will be interested to hear them and will probably tell others. These stories are based on true events but are so far-fetched and randomly selected that you'd think they were made up for the purpose of this site. With two books of the same content under his belt, these stories of useless information are proving to be more useful to him than he thought.

http://home.nycap.rr.com/useless/index.html

★ ★

:: MOTHER OF ALL EXCUSES

As long as there is authority, there will always be the need for excuses. These are normally used in one form or another to get oneself out of the proverbial doo-doo. Excuses usually work in the workplace, no matter how outrageous or unbelievable because it is unethical to call your staff liars when you have no way of proving it. In my opinion, the more far-fetched the excuse, the more likely it is that no one will ever question you. So here it is, the mother-of-all-excuses website. Page upon page of every excuse you could ever dream to muster up will keep you intrigued for hours. Just don't let the boss find out about it.

http://madtbone.tripod.com

★ ★

DEATH AND THE AFTERLIFE

ONE THING WE can be sure of is that one day we will die. That can be said with a definite amount of certainty. What happens to us once we have passed has always been an open-ended discussion, and I expect will remain a topic for debate for many years to come. As humans, we seek comfort in the reassurance that, once we're dead, our souls will live on, making the whole experience less final. But many believe that, when your body dies, you die and there is nothing more after that. Most of us get a fair old crack at life and, if we're honest, we should be grateful of the rest. But those who are seen to be taken before their time are thought to have a different purpose, and it's the idea of the afterlife that makes the harsh reality of a loved one's sudden departure all the easier to deal with. In this chapter, we touch on everything from a light-hearted look at death, through the serious side and all that's involved emotionally, to a just plain sick and demented look at the afterlife. I guess we all deal with death in different ways, some more unusual than others.

:: CORPSES FOR SALE

A very creepy website, which you may be put off entering just by hearing the name alone – unless of course you were looking to purchase a corpse, in which case I'm sure you'll be elated to hear about this little gem. The corpses are predominantly made of latex, which according to the site gives a realistic feel. You can custom-design your corpse to include flashing eyes, hair and skin colour and the degree of decay. View the images of the 'corpses' in various poses and outfits to get a feel for how your purchase will look once you get it home. All the realness of a rotting corpse but without the smell – the perfect lifelong companion.

http://www.distefano.com

★ ★

:: THE REINCARNATION STATION

There are many spiritual people in the world who believe in reincarnation. This term is widely known to be what happens to your spirit in the 'next life'. What you come back as strongly depends on your thoughts, morals and behaviour in this life. It's called karma. If you have been a saintly character living an honest and virtuous life then you will return in your next life as a powerful, well-respected higher being. However, if you have lived your life full of hate and sin you will return as a much lower life form, doomed to walk the Earth alone. Here is your chance to determine what fate has in store for you and whether you have done enough up until now to save yourself from yet another life of misery and despair.

http://www.reincarnationstation.com

★ ★

:: THE DEATH CLOCK

For all you impatient people out there who hate surprises and always need to be the first to hear about everything, this is the site for you. The Death Clock will predict, to the second, when you will die by gathering vital information about your date of birth, gender, weight, health and outlook on life. Save your personal death clock as a screensaver and start counting down the minutes of your life while you still can. Plan your life right up to your death so that none of your precious time left on Earth is wasted on wondering when you're going to croak.

http://www.deathclock.com

★ ★

:: GRAVE RIDES

What better way to live on the edge and tempt fate than by hiring a hearse to drive around in? This unique car-rental company have a fleet of customised hearses for all your transport needs. They even come with their own creepy chauffeur and coffin – with or without skeleton! Send your loved ones' hearts racing by surprising them with a trip in a 'Crypt de Ville' or paint the town red with a group of friends. Personally, I wouldn't be caught dead in one.

http://www.graverides.com

★ ★

:: WHAT LIES BENEATH

An online graveyard of the famous, infamous and just plain dead. Beneath Los Angeles is a website where you can visit hundreds of graveyards in the greater Los Angeles area. Have you always wanted to pay your respects to your favourite Hollywood movie star by visiting their final resting place? Well, now you can and it won't cost you an arm and a leg to get there. Just simply put their name in the search engine and if they were buried within the vicinity of the site you will be able to view their grave and pay respect to your hero. A nice idea, if not a little out of the ordinary, especially since you're invited to vote for your best grave.

http://www.beneathlosangeles.com

★ ★

:: BURY ME RIGHT

Do you revel in the idea of organising things such as parties, diet, work and what your partner wears? Are you the type who won't let anyone do anything for you? Then it's only proper that you should have total control over your final resting place and all that is involved in the process. Bury Me Right is a website where you can make all these arrangements online to ensure your special day doesn't die on its arse. Register with them and have total freedom over how you want your funeral to be, taking the stress away from your families, who will evidently have enough on their plate dealing with your passing. Go your own way and in style so that you will be remembered for the control freak you always were.

http://www.burymeright.com

★ ★

:: CELEBRITY MORGUE

Now, before we continue, I must warn you that there are pictures of real corpses on this site and links to some other morbid places that I will not be mentioning. The idea that celebrities will never be free from prying eyes has never been truer. Even in their resting state they can still be followed by their adoring fans in some kind of morbid act of celebrity perversion. Are they living out their final stage of what they signed up for when they became public phenomena, or are websites like this purely to satisfy a desperate world of voyeuristic weirdoes? I know what I'd rather believe.

http://www.celebritymorgue.com

★ ★

:: CITY MORGUE GIFT SHOP

This website was started up by Mark Chiavaroli, who worked as a first-call driver for a mortuary transport company. You could say he has a mild obsession with death after marrying a former licensed embalmer whom he met through his line of work. Together they maintain this site, which aims to educate people in an entertaining way on the topic of death. If you're feeling brave, take the death tour, or visit the celebrity cemetery, where you can visit the tombs of the rich and famous. And of course, staying true to its name, it will sell you novelty items such as the 'Men of Mortuaries' calendar or your very own personalised toe tag for when you finally cross over to the other side.

http://www.citymorguegiftshop.com

★ ★

:: DIE SCREAMING WITH SHARP THINGS IN YOUR HEAD

An odd little site to say the least, and I'm still trying to figure out its purpose. What I have concluded from viewing the pages several times is that it has no real purpose. It's merely a website containing pictures of domestic garden gnomes who have all been put to rest, screaming of course, with sharp things in their head! Why? I hear you ask. Why not? You can sign up if you wish and be the first to know when a new dying gnome has been added. I say the first because I can't actually imagine that anybody has signed up to this site, although I am probably wrong.

http://www.bifrost.com.au/hosting/gnomes

★ ★

:: GIRLS AND CORPSES

Just the sound of the two put together is enough for anyone to prick up their ears, whatever their thoughts on either subject. *Girls and Corpses* is an online magazine that combines the two in a way that enables guys to get off on the women and necrophiliacs to get off on the corpses. Whatever the underlying object of this magazine is, I don't think we'll ever really know, but its title alone is enough to stop Internet surfers in their tracks and take a peek into a world where they are turned on and sickened both at the same time.

http://www.girlsandcorpses.com

★ ★

:: AFTERLIFE TELEGRAMS

When a loved one crosses over to the spirit world we often take comfort in the thought that they are watching over us, protecting us and are with us in spirit, guiding us throughout our lives. Making contact with these spirits has always been a debatable topic of conversation. The creators of this website feel they have the answer to this ongoing discussion in the form of afterlife telegrams. For a 'donation' of $5 per word, you can send a message to a loved one in the spirit world via a terminally ill person, who memorises the message and delivers it to them after they die. An interesting idea with potentially groundbreaking results – let's just hope our messenger ends up on the right side of the Pearly Gates.

http://www.afterlifetelegrams.com

★ ★

:: MODERN MUMMIFICATION

The discussion of death is a tough one for many, and most people fear the subject and will avoid talking about it altogether. But we all know that the inevitable will one day be upon us and we must at some point give some thought to what will happen to our body once we do pass away. Modern Mummification is a way for your loved ones to continue to have you around even when you're gone, and is a novel way of dressing up the front room. Go it alone or take your beloved pet with you and be reunited once again in your afterlife.

http://www.summum.org/mummification

★ ★

:: LOOKING FOR A GRAVE?

This is your online guide to gravestones around the world. Are you struggling to locate a specific gravestone, cemetery or celebrity resting place? Well, you've come to the right place. This site, which I like to refer to as the Afterlife Yellow Pages – or Black Pages, if you prefer – will lead you to numerous cemeteries and gravestones worldwide. You can even search back through your ancestors and learn about your heritage. Sign up to this website and add your own family members who have passed on, making this one of the largest online networking site for the deceased. Watch out, MySpace, these guys are on to you.

http://www.findagrave.com

★ ★

:: ONLINE GRAVEYARD

My Cemetery is an online graveyard where you can secure your loved one's plot by submitting pictures of them so that they will have an online resting place where you can pay your respects from the comfort of your own terminal. To keep their memory alive, you can leave personal messages in the form of letters, poems, stories or pictures, and you are also invited to leave a 'letter from beyond' – while still in the land of the living, you can write a letter to your family and friends for them to remember you by when you're gone. A thoughtful but emotional site that shouldn't be read by hormonal females or males who have just seen their football team lose.

http://www.mycemetery.com

★ ★

:: RAPTURE LETTER

This is a website for all devout Christians hoping to meet up with their nearest and dearest again in the afterlife. What this site aims to provide is a message to your family and friends when you die, informing them first of your passing, and, second, of the possibilities Christianity can have in store for them in the next life. Now I'm not trying to push religion on to anybody: I'm merely opening your eyes to all the goings-on around the world no matter *what* your beliefs. In order for people to find out about this, you will need to submit the email addresses of all the people you want notified following your departure from this world and they will receive a computer-generated message informing them of your passing and also enticing them into the world of Christianity. What happened to a good old séance and a Ouija board?

http://www.raptureletters.com

★ ★

:: TOP-EARNING DEAD CELEBRITIES

Celebrities are more likely to make money from the grave than when they were alive. With their estates ever growing in value and their legacy living on, it seems from a celebrity point of view that the real bucks start rolling in once you've sung your last song or spoken your last line. View the current lucky 13, which features the top-earning dead celebrities from each year. Not surprisingly, names such as Kurt Cobain and Elvis Presley are top of the list, with earnings of $50 million and $42 million, respectively. You'll be sickened to know that the minimum earnings per annum to feature on this list is a whopping $7 million, which means they are still providing for their family even from the grave. They must have done *something* good in a past life. No rest for the wicked, eh?

http://www.forbes.com/2006/10/23/tech-media_06deadcelebs_cx_pk_top-earning-dead-celebrities_land.html

★ ★

∷ UNDERGROUND PARIS

This website takes you on a virtual tour of the tombs that lie directly below some of the most popular streets in Paris. This is the so-called resting place of more than 17 million Parisians whose skeletal remains were disinterred from past and present graveyards and are now neatly stacked to form the walls of the one-kilometre walk through the underpass. A scary insight into how we all may end up due to overpopulation over the centuries, making us question people when they talk of our *final* resting place. Take the surreal but worthwhile tour of the underground crypt and read up on the history of its origins. You'll be amazed at how well hidden it is, like a forgotten world of the very people who built the city they remain in.

http://triggur.org/cata/index.html

★ ★

:: DEATH, THE LAST TABOO

This is a website that is not afraid of death, or to speak openly about it. After all, it's the only thing in this world that we can categorically, 100 per cent for certain, say is going to happen (apart from taxes, of course) to each and every one of us at some point in our lives, and this site aims to explore people's taboos on the subject and how we deal with facing up to it. Read about people's fears of being buried alive and the inventors who created the safety coffins to prevent this, and view the face masks of moulds taken minutes after people have passed away to show their final expression. Is this the wake-up call we need, facing death head on in order for us to accept it? Or are we happy remaining ignorant of the inevitable?

http://www.deathonline.net

★ ★

:: LIFE GEM

Does the thought of losing someone close to you drive you to despair? Can't imagine living without that special person in your life and would like to see them continue on life's path with you as something beautiful and valuable? Life Gem can make this happen. With special technology they are able to take carbon from a lock of hair and use it to create an everlasting diamond of your choice. You can treasure this timeless piece of jewellery for ever and pass it down through the generations as a reminder of their heritage. My only query is, what happens if it gets lost or damaged? Presumably nothing. But, hey, at least you'll still have your memories.

http://www.lifegem.com

★ ★

:: ADIPOCERE

Have you started to plan your funeral and have already requested a traditional burial? This website may just put you off, because it holds a multitude of information on adipocere, otherwise known as grave wax. This is the insoluble fatty acids left as residue from pre-existing fats from decomposing flesh that often carries a cheese-like odour that can be found on most if not all corpses as a part of the decomposition process. Visit this site for a detailed look into the detailed world of adipocere in the form of its history and scientific breakdown. After viewing this site with its gory descriptions and graphic pictures, you'll be queuing for the furnace and probably running to the nearest toilet.

http://adipocere.homestead.com

★ ★

LANGUAGE AND LITERATURE

THE INTERNET HAS become a breeding ground for language overs and, with plenty of ways to challenge language, many websites have taken on the role of giving people some light relief in the form of generators, dictionaries and translators. This chapter shows that language can be entertaining, and, if used in a diplomatic way, can bring different societies, cultures and races together. People's attitudes to language can be quite diverse and often meet conflicts of opinions. What many of these websites portray is how there can be no right or wrong answers when it comes to language and that its meaning actually comes from the way we interpret it.

:: THE KLINGON LANGUAGE INSTITUTE

Have you always felt left out of the group when your friends start speaking a strange language that you've never heard of? No, I'm not talking about French, but about Klingon. This is the native tongue of those bumpy-headed aliens from *Star Trek* and this is their site to help spread their language across the world. Here's where you can learn all about the galaxy's fastest-growing language and join millions of other Klingon conversers in topical sci-fi debates. So what are you waiting for, go on and *lojmIt yIpoSmoH*! (It means open the door!)

http://www.kli.org

★ ★

:: PRISONERS' DICTIONARY

Language is ever evolving due to movement of people from different countries and areas. Prison culture is much the same, if not more so, as the number of people passing in and out of institutions from different countries, cities and cultures leads to diversity in language trends. Prisoners will have select words or sayings that they use to replace things that already have given names, mostly used as code words to stop the authorities finding out what they're saying, but also in day-to-day conversations. With the constant movement of people through these prisons, words and phrases continue to get manipulated or updated so it's hard to keep a static log of the most recent words. This website aims to portray some of the terms used in today's prisons where English is the first language of most of the inmates.

http://dictionary.prisonwall.org

★ ★

:: CUSS CONTROL

If you're the type of hothead who doesn't know when to keep his mouth shut and often lets his emotions get the better of him, then you should pay attention to this site. It will not only teach you how to stop using profanities but will also help you to think positively and not get so worked up in heated situations. This group of anti-swearers have created a website to tame the tongues of all you foul-mouthed cursers. Follow their ten helpful hints to gaining a cleaner gob, and a more pleasant temper in the process. A website that makes you stop and think before opening your mouth. Bloody brilliant!

http://www.cusscontrol.com

★ ★

:: ENGLISH BLOOPERS

This is a website dedicated to misprints by people for whom English is not their first language. Have you ever been abroad and chuckled to yourself when the waiter brings you a menu and one of the items is misspelled, and has become a rude or funny word? Well, if that got you going, check out this site dedicated to such mistakes. This is the sort of site that would drive hardcore grammatical boffins crazy, because there are loads of incorrect spellings and misused words within these pages. So grab yourself a can of Cock and check out the archive section for a closer look at bloopers from around the world.

http://www.englishbloopers.com/index.html

★ ★

:: MISUSED QUOTATION MARKS

For some, seeing quotation marks used incorrectly is as 'annoying' as trying to sleep while a persistent mosquito 'buzzes' around their ear. The creators of this website know this only too well and this is their chance to put all the quotation-mark 'wrongs' that they have witnessed to 'rights'. Read through a plethora of 'examples' ranging from the funny to the painfully obvious and either revel in your knowledge for understanding the 'errors', or start to 'educate' yourself before these 'anal perfectionists' come and 'hunt' you down.

http://www.juvalamu.com/qmarks

★ ★

:: IDIOMS

Have you ever wondered about the origins of sayings that you may use on a day-to-day basis? This website alphabetically lists hundreds of idioms that are used daily, and a detailed description of what each saying means. Some you'll be surprised at, while others will be more obvious, but either way they will bring a whole new meaning to the term 'think before you speak', because now you will actually understand what you're saying rather than just talking out of your backside. If you liked these little beauties check out http://www.oxymoronlist.com, a neighbouring site that has more or less the same effect.

http://www.idiomsite.com

★ ★

:: READ IT, SWAP IT

Do you see yourself as something of a bookworm but hate having hundreds of books lying about your house? This website is here to combat this problem for you by allowing you to read a book and, once finished with it, swap it for another. Now you may think this sounds like an online library. Well, you're absolutely right, except that, rather than borrow the library's books, you donate your own books in return for someone else's, and the pattern keeps continuing among different users. A clever way to get everyone reading books without the added expense – and is environmentally friendly too!

http://www.readitswapit.co.uk

★ ★

:: SPELLING BEE

Spelling bees in the US are more than kids having to stand up in assembly and being tested on how to spell hard words because they've been talking through the headteacher's morning speech. They are a serious mind sport and thousands of kids across America's states vigorously train and prepare for the crown. These beauty pageants for brainiacs are so demanding that their participants are confined to hours of rigorous mind-conditioning training to prepare their brains. This website is here for competitors and their parents to get up-to-date information on all the spelling-bee competitions taking place and the best resources for studying the craft. Read through previous results to see how the competition sizes up, allowing competitors to prepare mentally for their next performance, or visit the online store for all the latest books and souvenirs on the sport.

http://www.spellingbee.com

★ ★

:: THE ALTERNATIVE DICTIONARY

One of the novelties of going abroad as a child was to come back and show off to your friends that you could say rude words in another language, and admittedly some adults still to this day have a little giggle at this pastime. This website will save you years of travelling, as it's all listed here, alphabetically for your amusement. With 162 different languages and 2,743 different profanities to choose from, you can continue your playground antics at friends' parties, bringing an edge of diversity to the table.

http://www.notamo2.no/~hcholm/altlang

★ ★

:: THE DIALECT CONVERTER

Have you ever wondered what it would be like to be able to speak another dialect? Or maybe you are a budding writer who can't seem to get the right edge to your work. This website is host to the 'Dialectizer', which literally converts your Queen's English websites and creative-writing text into different dialects of your choice. Give your Christmas cards a cockney edge, or your DIY website a redneck character. Other amusing options are to view other more serious sites in one of these different dialects, adding a bit of fun where the boring-doctor has been.

http://www.rinkworks.com/dialect

★ ★

:: THE FORBIDDEN LIBRARY

This website holds a library of books that have been banned or challenged in some way due to the nature of their content. Find out why a classroom book about censorship got censored and why the renowned children's author Roald Dahl has been seen to promote drugs and disobedience. Scroll through the endless reasons why these books were banned – for example, *The Diary of Anne Frank* because in 1983 members of the Alabama State Textbook Committee said it was a 'real downer' – and follow the links to purchase the forbidden books to find out whether you agree with the comments that got them banned.

http://www.forbiddenlibrary.com

★ ★

:: WORD ASSOCIATION

Unless you have at least 20 minutes to spare, I suggest you don't look at this website. At first glance, it may look very easy to resist, but as soon as you enter your first word into the database you'll be hooked. The idea behind this site is to play a game of word association, the lonely generator will entice you to play by giving you a word, and your job is to type in the first word that comes to your head, it will then give you one back and so on. Originally set up as an experiment, this website now holds more than 54,658 words and 4,800,483 associations between these words. I challenge you to beat the generator – you never will.

http://www.wordassociation.org

★ ★

:: REVERSE SPEECH

The 1980s introduced us to the concept of hidden messages within songs. Several high-profile rock'n'roll groups were being accused of trying to communicate with their fans by using lyrics that, if played backwards, sounded as if they were trying to corrupt the minds of their impressionable admirers. Much speculation surrounded this subject, since it could be argued that it was merely a coincidence or the misinterpretation of several right-wing protestors, or that the artists were out to brainwash their loyal followers. Either way, the idea of reverse speech hasn't died down over the decades and this site is dedicated to the study and its significance in modern-day culture. Judge for yourself by listening to examples and reading up on whether it is subconsciously part of our natural speech process, or whether it's all a load of paranoia-induced rubbish.

http://www.reversespeech.com

★ ★

MEDIA AND POPULAR CULTURE

DUE TO THE vast number of Internet users on a daily basis, the World Wide Web has fast become the number-one medium for reaching out to the masses on a maximum-exposure level. It is due to this very fact that artists, performers and celebrity figures all now capitalise on the advantages of the Internet for their own personal gain. With networking sites such as MySpace and Facebook, people are launching careers from their bedrooms, and are able to generate fan bases all on their own without the need of management or media deals. This chapter shows how the Internet is used as a vital tool in today's media world and how, if you're not a part of it, you'll get left behind.

:: MAKE ME A STAR!

Most young children dream of growing up to become a famous pop-star, actor or sports personality, but few actually make it to that top spot. Some would say it's down to talent alone, while others think it's a matter of being in the right place at the right time. Either way, those who are really determined won't give up until they see their name in lights – and this website holds an army of those future would-be stars. I Wanna Be Famous was set up to allow budding stars to showcase themselves on a website that claims to be viewed by millions worldwide and has accumulated plenty of press interest to date. Create your profile by submitting either a picture or video clip of yourself and explain why you want to be famous, then just sit tight and hope that some great industry guru will stumble across your profile and sign you up to make your dreams come true.

http://www.iwannabefamous.com

★ ★

:: BIG BUBBLE

Far more interesting than watching paint dry, Big Bubble is an online reality show that unlike its competitors runs 24 hours a day, 365 days of the year. Watch the live streaming direct from the tank and catch up with all the latest news and gossip about the tank mates. Within the tank there are two live tank cams to choose between and you can even watch past footage of the tank mates talking to Big Bubble in the diary tank. View nominations and choose who you want to get the scoop, or find out whether your favourite has swum or managed to survived another week in the tank. Who goes? You decide!

http://www.bigbrother.co.uk

★ ★

:: BLACK ELVIS

Everyone loves an entertainer for their weddings, parties and corporate events, which is why Colbert Hamilton has decided to turn his talents to the lucrative market of the tribute act. London-based Hamilton has been performing on the music circuit for many years now. Originally the front man for a rockabilly band, he has now honed his talents to become the UK's original Black Elvis. Visit his website to listen to samples of his work, book him for an event or find out where he will be playing next. One thing's for sure: the King lives on!

http://www.blackelvis.co.uk

★ ★

:: SKIN IN THE MOVIES

Welcome to the dermatology-in-the-cinema website, which looks at the skin conditions of A-list celebrities in blockbuster movies. The science on this site looks at three main categories: actors with skin problems, villains with problem skin and movie roles that require realistic skin makeup. Moles, birthmarks, tattoos, rashes, hair loss, scars and genetic disorders all get checked out in a regular analysis of a huge range of movies. *The Da Vinci Code*, *Harry Potter* and *The X Men* all get dissected.

http://www.skinema.com

★ ★

:: DUKE

This website is home to three alternative musicians who are collectively known as Duke. Formed in 2005, having met through a shared love of improvised music, Duke have spread their sound across the world via festivals, tours and supporting other renowned groups. With only a guitar for an instrument, they create the rest of the sound through the vocal talents of two members making up the beat, baseline, tune and vocals. Check out their equally diverse website, where you'll get a tour of their world through interactive icons.

http://www.dukelive.co.uk

★ ★

:: ED WOOD

This is the church of the late cult director Edward D Wood Jr. Woodism is a pop-culture-based religion created in 1996 by Reverend Steve Galindo, intended to use Ed and his films to inject spirituality into those who get little fulfilment from more mainstream religions. With more than three thousand followers of the movement, it's proving to be more than just a celebration of the late director and his quirkiness but more a way of life and example to its people. Learn the holy lessons of Wood or get an online baptism for all hard-core followers.

http://www.edwood.org

★ ★

:: NAKED NEWS

What better way to start your day than to turn on your computer and watch the daily news headlines presented by a fleet of naked female reporters? Well, that's just what this website is offering you. Subscription to the site does come at a cost, but these robeless reporters promise to give you up-to-date news stories from around the world with an added bonus: they're naked! Watch the free video to get a taster of what's to come and be surprised by the girls' professional attitude to their work, so much so that after a while you end up forgetting they are starkers and focus on the actual topics being reported. A groundbreaking website that really knows its market, proving that nakedness and news really can go hand in hand, giving its viewers some light relief from all the upheaval in the world.

http://www.nakednews.com

★ ★

:: PROSTHETIC JUSTICE

This website pays tribute to false limbs and the like and celebrates their roles in the world of entertainment. Throughout the centuries, audiences have been entertained by celebrity personalities and their friendly sidekicks in a host of different acts, including ventriloquists, puppets and extra limbs. Learn from the experts all the tricks of the trade and sing along with the Rolf Harris classic 'Jake the Peg'. Let us not forget Bernie Clifton and his world-famous ostrich and the late Rod Hull and his mischievous Emu. Entertainment at its finest – they don't make 'em like they used to.

http://www.prosthetic-justice.2om.com/index.html

★ ★

:: LOINCLOTHS

One for the ladies or those with a penchant for Hollywood hunks cavorting around in loincloths, this site hosts a handful of barely clothed male pinups for you to salivate over. View them in many different forms from the young, the old, the famous and the not so famous. Read up on the origins of the loincloth and without stating the obvious why they attract so much attention. Browse through this site to view these scantily clad males performing different activities such as acting and modelling, or, for a better insight, spy on them hunting or climbing trees.

http://www.karstensloinclothsite.com

★ ★

:: LIVE LEAK

This website depicts all the crazy goings-on in the world that the mainstream media may not want you to see. Live Leak allows its viewers to send in news stories and video footage that they feel would be of public interest, giving the site viewers up-to-date news on real issues from around the world. This site offers an alternative angle that the public can relate to without feeling as if they were being given a biased slant from a higher power. View hilarious news videos that you weren't supposed to see and breaking news stories from across the world. A must-see site for people who love to see a good Bush bashing.

http://www.liveleak.com

★ ★

:: MOVIE MISTAKES

Film and TV buffs often have a morbid fascination with watching actors screw up their lines, and seeing dodgy sets wobble, so much so that programmes showing outtakes that you weren't supposed to see are made in their honour. This website runs along the same lines. It's an online archive of movie mistakes, mostly depicting questionable scene changes and continuity screw-ups. Find out which blockbuster movies contained the most mistakes and view them in video and still format, or if you've noticed any film *faux pas* that this site hasn't, you are invited to send them in for all to scrutinise.

http://www.moviemistakes.com

★ ★

:: NAME THAT PORNO

Porn-movie titles are often a cheeky play on words or spoof title of a critically acclaimed film. This website invites you daily to turn a popular film title into a smutty porno name. It's surprisingly harder than it looks, and participants should have an eye for lewdness and a love of bad puns with a no-holds-barred attitude to create the most titillating titles to lure in the filthiest of minds. The less creative among you can still make use of this site by voting for your favourite title of the day. Possibly the best area of the site is the no-change-necessary section, where aptly named films are ready to roll with their porno remake – *Howards End*, *Dick Tracy* and *Batteries Not Included* are a few choice favourites.

http://www.namethatporno.com

★ ★

:: WEIRD NEWS
All the weirdness of the world is listed here in up-to-the-minute breaking-news stories. With so many topical subjects to cover in the mainstream media today, offbeat stories too often get overlooked. This is your chance to catch up on all the abnormalities of the world and be the first to find out about fascinating stories that you otherwise wouldn't hear about.

http://www.travellady.biz/coolstuff/weirdnews.htm
http://www.crazypress.net

★ ★

:: OFFICIAL DOGGY POO

This is the official website of a lovable character, Doggy Poo. Read the heart-rending tale of his struggle to become accepted and his quest to be a useful entity in this world. Meet his philosophical friends, Leaf, Flower, Mother Hen and Soil, who teach him the qualities of life. The original story came from the Korean writer Jung-Saeng Kwon in 1968 and was brought to the big screen by director Oh-Sung Kwon in 2003. If you're one of those who take a shine to the lovable Mr Poo, you can further your support by watching the movie trailer or by purchasing the full-length movie and soundtrack in the online store.

http://www.doggypooworld.com

★ ★

:: SCRUMPDILLYSHUS LAND

A seriously entertaining site that is the visual playground behind the Bran Flakes musical world. The Bran Flakes are a team of alternative-music producers who take samples from nostalgic music of the past and use it to create new music of their own. It's unlike anything you've heard before. The creators of this sound have come up with a kitsch interactive site where they can show off their musical masterpieces in a visually complementary way.

There's a fun, if not a slightly eerie, feel about this site, but it's extremely addictive and you'll find yourself pressing buttons for hours.

http://www.thebranflakes.com/scrump/frameset.html

★ ★

:: SWEET CHILDHOOD

Some celebrities aren't content with producing popularity through their talent alone and often capitalise on their private lives to generate more publicity for themselves. This website homes in on this subject and, with the use of psychologists, psychiatrists and other professionals working in these fields, it aims to predict the psychological damage and dysfunction that the children of these celebrities may suffer as a result of their parents' actions. Poor little things!

http://www.fadetoblack.com/children

★ ★

:: MOVIE CLICHÉS

Have you ever watched a movie and thought to yourself, I've seen that done before? Or maybe the thing that you're seeing wouldn't necessarily happen in everyday life but is always depicted in the same clichéd way on the big screen. This website pays homage to those moments, listing the most annoying and common logic flaws and stereotypes found in movies. Browse through pages of alphabetically listed clichés and remind yourself just how predictable the world of film can be. Many directors seem to follow this pattern for fear that their audience won't be able to relate to the film, so it takes a truly talented director to steer clear of these stereotypes and still portray the message to their viewers.

http://www.moviecliches.com

★ ★

:: THIS IS TRUE

'This is True' is a weekly syndicated newspaper column by American writer Randy Cassingham. The website reports on unbelievable but true news items that Cassingham researches daily from reputable newspapers around the world depicting all the bizarre goings-on for your amazement and ends with a final word from the columnist. Subscribe to this website and receive your weekly bout of bizarre global news delivered straight to your inbox.

http://www.thisistrue.com

★ ★

:: THE SECRET

This one claims to reveal to you the great Secret of the universe in the form of a feature-length movie. The film supposedly reveals to its fortunate viewers the key to unlimited joy, health, money, relationships, love, youth and everything you have ever wanted. The Secret is the culmination of many centuries of great thinkers, scientists, artists and philosophers and the creative minds of Prime Time Productions, the people who put this project together. Watch the trailer online and, if you are intrigued and wish to know more, you can download the full-length movie, or buy the DVD online. If you happen to find out what the Secret is, do me a favour and let me know.

http://thesecret.tv

★ ★

:: WICKED TALENT

This is an online model agency with a difference. Log on to this site if you are searching for that special someone to spice up your upcoming events, productions and shows, or if you simply want to ogle the strange and macabre. These models, actors and performers all dare to be different and are there to showcase their unique flair. They excel in being distinctive and are waiting for that lucky break that will lead to bigger and better opportunities than the usual run-of-the-mill talent-agency books can offer. As the late great Mae West once said, 'It's better to be looked over than overlooked.'

http://www.wickedtalent.net

★ ★

:: CELEB MATCH

Have you ever fancied yourself as the next Mrs Brad Pitt, or maybe you feel you are destined to get intimate with Cameron Diaz. OK, so it's likely that this will never happen, but this online test could prove that, given different circumstances, should your two paths intertwine, you just might be compatible. What this site aims to do is work out both your and your fantasy partner's biorhythms to see if in an ideal world you would be a perfect pair. This test also works on normal citizens, too, so, if you have a secret crush on your next-door neighbour or you just want to see how well matched you and your current partner are, give it a whirl. Remember, it's only a game, so don't start doing table plans just yet!

http://www.celebmatch.com

★ ★

:: I'M NOT A CELEBRITY, GET ME IN THERE!

Some people are so desperate for fame that they will go to any lengths necessary to get them to the top spot. This website is an attempt to propel non-celebrity figure Mark into a household name overnight. Cemetery supervisor Mark has been trying his hand at the fame game virtually all his life, and his rejection from a reality-TV talent show because he wasn't able to sing led him to create this site. His ambition is to get on to ITV's hit reality-TV show *I'm a Celebrity, Get Me Out of Here*, but the main thing stopping him from realising this dream is that he's not yet a celebrity. Through this site, he hopes to create a following that will propel him to Internet celebrity status, thus making him 'eligible' as a contestant on the show. Follow his online antics and show your support – he's going to need it.

http://www.freewebs.com/imnotacelebritygetmeinthere

★ ★

RACE AND RELIGION

ONE OF MANY things that the Internet allows people to do is to stand on their virtual soapboxes and vent their opinions to a waiting audience. As long as race and religion are a part of society, people will always be vocal and opinionated on these subjects. In this chapter, you will witness outspoken views from various groups and organisations who all wish to voice their opinion within this subject matter. Prepare to be shocked, amused and outraged at the content of these sites showing just how controversial race and religion are.

:: THE BRICK TESTAMENT

This website illustrates the Bible with the use of the holiest form of building bricks, Lego. Created by the unordained Rev. Brendan Powell Smith, this site gives insight into Bible stories that are made easy to understand due to its straightforward animations. With 268 stories and 3,048 illustrations to date, the Rev. has certainly kept himself busy. Catch his work online or buy one of his three illustrated books, all spreading the message of the Lord in the form of Lego-oriented art. And, in the interests of parents who wish to educate their children through the means of this site, each story comes complete with a rating guide so you can protect their innocent eyes from any nudity, sexual content, violence and swearing – how reassuring.

http://www.thebricktestament.com

★ ★

:: ANAL SEX ACCORDING TO GOD

This highly controversial site provides answers to unmarried Christians on the topic of abstinence. Read through their guide to what they depict as God's will and either be outraged or amused by the advice on offer. Married couples don't need to feel left out, either, since there are plenty of sexual adventures for you on this site too. A warning, though, to the virginal and sexually inexperienced: this site contains shocking verbal content, but supposedly they have the backing of God, so it can't all be sinful, can it?

http://www.sexinchrist.com

★ ★

:: BLACK PEOPLE LOVE US!

This website is supposedly brought to you by a middle-class white couple who go by the names of Sally and Johnny. This is probably one of the funniest websites that I have come across depicting the stereotypes of modern-day culture. The site is based on the couple's love for black people and their passion to share this with the world. Read through some of the most shockingly amusing pages of this site, which to me not only highlights how society is more comfortable with confronting issues of race and culture, but also points out that people's prejudice *between* races will always be around, whether it's portrayed in a negative or positive way. The clever thing that this site manages to do is invite its viewers to email in their comments and, in doing this, it turns the attention round to the prejudices of those who write in, giving the true answer to how society views the issue of race, religion and culture. Judge for yourself whether this site is for real or not and admire the balls it took to create it.

http://www.blackpeopleloveus.com

★ ★

:: EVIL BIBLE?

This website has some extremely opinionated views on God and the Bible and its effect on society through the centuries. It depicts many contradictions that they have found within the Holy Book and have brought them to the attention of all who view this site. The Bible holds many different interpretations of God's words that have been speculated on since its creation, and, with statistics showing the number of people turning their backs on religion, we can see that the number only increases. I guess the true question is what we are able to learn from websites like these, and what they hope to achieve by revealing these so-called truths of the Bible.

http://www.evilbible.com

★ ★

:: GOD CHECKER

This is the website to visit if you want up-to-date information surrounding all the various gods of religion and spirituality. Its impressive library boasts around 2,850 deities with a description on the history and practice within each movement. The site creators themselves don't pretend to have the answers to all religious questions and are just as inquisitive about learning the truths about the gods, so, if you feel that they have left your master out or wish to inform them on any inaccuracies that you may have witnessed on their site, they will be more than accommodating in listening to your request. How very godlike indeed!

http://www.godchecker.com

★ ★

:: THE BIBLE IN PIG LATIN

Many people who attempt to read the Bible find it can be a tall order understanding all of the scripture. This website, a link from the Museum of Conceptual Art homepage, attempts either to confuse us further or give us an easier way to read the Holy Book by translating the text into pig Latin. If you're familiar with pig Latin, it will be a novel way of reading the words that have graced the holy pages for centuries and will help readers, who are maybe bored with the original text, get a feel for the Good Book again. For those who are unfamiliar with pig Latin, where have you been hiding? Follow this link – http://www.idiomasoftware.com/pig/pig_latin.html – which will give a full breakdown of how to understand the common dialect to enhance your time with God and make it a whole new experience.

http://www.museumofconceptualart.com/ible-bay.html

★ ★

:: THE CULT CONSTRUCTION SET

This website sums up the vulnerability of society's attitudes towards religion today. You are invited to create your own cult and they even help you along the way by giving you ideas in the form of actions and practices that your group will stand by. With so many controversial minds and people of power, the public are fed conflicting information on what's right and wrong every day, creating a nation of paranoid people searching for an alternative outlet. This site highlights the need in people to break free from the constraints of modern-day society and go it alone with their own trains of thought and practices.

http://www.fadetoblack.com/cultkit

★ ★

:: THE POPE'S CONFESSIONAL PAGE

Have you been harbouring a secret and feel the need to get something off your chest? Visit this site and you'll get the release you've been craving in the form of the online confessional booth. Admittedly, the man posing as the Pope looks a little pervy to say the least – but, hey, at least he's up for listening! After spilling your guts out to this complete stranger, do what any normal nosey person would do and read up on every other troubled soul's confessions, too. I know they're private but some things are just too tempting to resist.

http://www.users.globalnet.co.uk/~dspope/marcuspope

★ ★

:: NOAH'S ARK

For three months in 1974 Pastor Richard Greene had been seeing visions of a large ark on a hillside and people from all over the world were travelling from far and wide to witness it. His dream started becoming a reality when he began believing that this was a message from God telling him to rebuild his congregation a new church as a replica of Noah's Ark. There is an interesting if not informative media clip detailing the project and a chance to hear Chosen One Greene speaking to his congregation, and you are also invited to visit the construction site where the Ark will one day stand.

http://www.godsark.org

★ ★

∷ JESUS CHRIST SUPERSTORE

This is the site where people from all walks of life can come and view as one, for the creators hold no prejudice towards your ethnic origins and followings. What started out as an exhibition is now a gallery of toys depicting different religious characters throughout history. Unfortunately, they are no longer available for sale but there are plans to produce more figures in the near future, so stay logged on.

http://www.jesuschristsuperstore.net

★ ★

NOSTALGIA

REMINISCING IS WHAT we humans do best to the extent that some people literally live for the past. Reflecting on days gone by will always be a favourite pastime of old school friends, work colleagues and students. It's the unobtainable passion with the past that we all pine for, remembering the good times we used to have back then when we were young and carefree. Nostalgia creeps up on us all the time, in every aspect of our lives. Whether it's through a song or movie, or just by going through an old photo album, we are constantly reminded of our past. In this chapter, you will find more past pleasures than anywhere else, sending you back in time to all the oddities you'd long forgotten. Gain an insight into why people pine for the past and how they make money from their favourite pastimes. Witness people's inabilities to let go and what lengths they will go to to keep the days of yesteryear firmly in the present, no matter how good or bad they really were.

:: THE VINTAGE VACUUM CLEANER

The vacuum cleaner is every modern-day housewife's best friend, and every modern-day feminist's worst enemy. Whether you love it or hate it, this friendly little site has all the facts on the sucker that loves to clean your house. Read through the phenomenal history of how the vacuum cleaner was created and take a step back in time to view images of different models used throughout the years. Those who are opposed to using a bit of elbow grease when it comes to housework might be interested, if they have the stomach for it, to find out what average household dirt actually consists of and see how fast those feminists run for that hoover!

http://www.137.com/museum

★ ★

:: EIGHTIES NOSTALGIA

Love this period or hate it, the 1980s provided us with a decade of flamboyance that will aid us in debates about its tastes for many more years to come. It was the arrogance of the people at the time that propelled fashion, music and design into a new dimension of overbearing chicness that was often hard to stomach. This website regurgitates the whole decade by serving you classic eighties material as obnoxious as ever in the form of TV, music and a whole host of nostalgic products that will have you digging out your BMX and rocking those shoulder pads.

http://www.8osnostalgia.com

★ ★

:: ANTIQUE WEIRDNESS

This website is brought to you by an avid antiques collector who goes by the name of Brian. What makes this site different from other collectors' sites is that the antiques and memorabilia he collects are something of the strange variety. With some real treats in store, you'll be hard pushed to find material like this anywhere else under one domain. There's even a racist section containing some politically incorrect material that once was unethically seen as entertainment – shame on those ignorant bigots!

http://home.teleport.com/~gumball/weird.html

★ ★

:: 20TH-CENTURY POP CULTURE

If it's 20th-century vintage items that you're after, this is the site for you. Do Wah Diddy was the brainchild of an American couple who couldn't afford to furnish their property with brand-new furniture, leading them to purchase items from flea markets and second-hand stores. They couldn't resist a bargain and ended up with more vintage junk than Camden Market. This sparked the idea to open a shop, which enabled them to carry on collecting their pastime treasures while making money out of it. They now have an online shop where you can purchase hundreds of original items that you're unlikely to find anywhere else on the Net, as well as their private warehouse, which avid collectors can visit by appointment only. Visit this site for a step back in time and very reasonably priced vintage merchandise.

http://www.dowahdiddy.com

★ ★

:: LONDON BUS PRESERVATION TRUST

Remember the time when smoking was allowed on buses? You had to hop on at the back of these old specimens, sometimes while they were moving, and a conductor walked up and down the bus collecting fares and giving out tickets. Take a step back in time with this nostalgic site as we learn the history of London buses through this quaint little museum. The London Bus Preservation Trust's commitment is to restore and preserve some of London's oldest buses dating back as early as 1923. Find out information about visiting the museum on one of its open days, or become a member and meet other London-bus enthusiasts and exchange tips on restoration projects.

http://www.lbpt.org

* *

:: DUBBIN

For those who are unfamiliar with the product dubbin, it is a natural wax-and-oil product that softens, conditions and makes all leather items waterproof. Dubbin was created over a hundred years ago and never has it been more appreciated than by the creator of this website. Discover its alternative uses and how it can be used for creative purposes, or read up on the true history of how dubbin was founded. For a deeper insight into how this product is generating publicity, view the gallery of celebrities who are all hardcore dubbin fans and sign up to *Dubbinews* for updates.

http://www.dubbin.com

* *

:: I USED TO BELIEVE

Most of us when growing up had overactive imaginations that would take us off to fantasy worlds that in reality didn't exist. We were young, imaginative and extremely gullible, and often believed in far-fetched stories and old wives' tales. As we get older, our minds become more conditioned to society and the letdowns of life, resulting in the loss of innocence and unspoiled qualities we had as children. This website depicts the childhood beliefs that we now know to be merely fantasy. Take a trip down Memory Lane and remember what it was like to have no mental hang-ups with the world.

http://www.iusedtobelieve.com

★ ★

∷ WOMEN AND DOGS

This online photo album has generated a multitude of media attention since its launch in the early 2000s simply because of its eccentric collection of women and dogs. Let's be honest, you'd be hard pushed in this day and age to surf the Internet for such a site without the corrupt minds of sex-crazed moneymakers' websites popping up first, which is why this site makes for a refreshing library of pictures that hold a history of their own. This website came about not from the creator's passion for women and dogs, but more an idea that came about due to a chance finding. The most captivating thing about this collection is the unanswered history that each photograph holds, a bit like a window to the past where you are invited to create the story. Kitsch and quirky, nostalgia at its finest!

http://www.womenanddogsuk.co.uk

★ ★

:: TELETEXT

This website celebrates the information provider that has been serving households across Britain since 1974. At one time it was the only live gateway to the outside world, but, with the launch of the Internet and digital TV, it's a wonder Teletext is still around. Refusing to revamp its archaic look could wipe it out altogether due to more contemporary and accessible digital outlets that are now a common feature in modern British homes. We all have at one time in our lives relied on the trusted information pages. Whether it was to look up the Friday-night TV or cinema listings or to book a budget holiday, it never failed to come up with the goods, giving its users up-to-the-minute information. My personal favourite was playing the general-knowledge game Bamboozle while waiting for something good to come on the four TV channels that were then available, and revelling in my discovery of the hold button instead of having to rush through all the text before the page changed. Ah, those were the days!

http://teletext.mb21.co.uk

★ ★

:: SWEET TEMPTATIONS

This is the ultimate online store for all your chocolate treats and will take you back to your childhood days of pre-filling, non-sensitive teeth. The creators of this retro site have hand-picked all your favourite playground swaps, enticing you into the past by temptingly displaying them. Browse through the collection to find your top treat as well as some that you may have missed out on. With everything from penny sweets to chocolate bars, you'll be piling on the pounds just viewing this site.

http://www.nostalgiccandy.com

★ ★

:: KIDS GAMES

Take another trip down Memory Lane with this website and reminisce about the games we used to play as kids. The playground will always be a strong school-day memory for most of us and the games we used to play there will often stick in our minds. Visit this site to remind you of the days when you actually enjoyed being outside in the cold damp weather and prayed that the end-of-break whistle would never get blown.

http://www.gameskidsplay.net

★ ★

:: PEZ, ANYONE?

The things that people collect and the lengths they will go to in order to get their collectables will always amaze me, as will their passion for it all. Do they start with a few items and think, Right, I'm now going to try to collect as many of these as I can and dedicate my working life to it? Or is it something they were born into, feel they inherited and believe they need to keep collecting to follow the family tradition? Whatever the answer, I admire their commitment and perseverance with their hobby, even if the items in question are a little odd. An example of this is the PEZ Exhibit website. Remember those sweet holders that had a different cartoon characters head as the opening? Well, this site is a collection of them. Be amazed by the number that were created and collected and are still being produced today.

http://www.spectrumnet.com/~spectrum/pez/pezexhibit.html

★ ★

:: RETRO DOLLS

This cool site is the home of a US designer and vintage-doll dresser who goes by the name of Liz Retro. Visit the pages of some of these elegantly dressed dollies, which you are now able to purchase and display in your home. With fashions from the forties through to the eighties, these little treasures are not to be used for your adult re-enactment of 'Mummies and Daddies', however hard the temptation may be.

http://hometown.aol.com/lizretros/dolls.html

★ ★

:: SAILOR JERRY

This website is dedicated to renowned sailor Norman 'Sailor Jerry' Collins (1911–73), whom many viewed as the father of body art in the form of tattooing. View a brief history of his life and the tales of how his body art became more than a fashion statement but a mark of his life and travels. From the opening of his first tattoo parlour in Honolulu's Chinatown, his memory lives on in stores worldwide, where you can buy merchandise and artwork and even get your own Sailor Jerry tattoo in his honour. A website for hardcore tattoo enthusiasts to gain a greater understanding into the history of the art form and why it is so popular today.

http://www.sailorjerry.com

★ ★

:: BAD FADS

Let's face it, we've all had fashion disasters that we wish we could forget, but the memories and photos keep coming back to haunt us. This website is the smack in the face that we all love to hate, since it takes us through a fashion time warp of all the clichés of an era. Browse through decades of red-carpet no-nos and remind yourself of how bad it once was, with this online time capsule of trends from the past.

http://www.badfads.com

★ ★

:: THEORIES ON GRIMACE

For those of you who are blissfully unaware of this character, I applaud you, since you are about to get your first lesson in how to use cuddly characters to entice children into fast food. Grimace is the lovable friend of Ronald McDonald and is widely used in the McDonald's marketing campaigns. As you will see from the images on this site, he is a purple cuddly creature with a kind nature, but is portrayed as being clumsy and a bit of a simple soul. Apart from that and his love of milkshakes, the site creators are still bamboozled by this character's existence. Read through a breakdown of other McDonald's characters and read up on the marketing theories of one of the largest fast-food chains in the world.

http://www.angelfire.com/mo/jogrimace

★ ★

:: I PITY THE FOOL!

This website was developed by two avid Mr T fans who have combined their personal collections to create one of the largest piles of Mr T memorabilia in the world. Mr T, born Laurence Tureaud, is best known for his role as 'BA' (standing for 'Big Attitude') Baracus in the 1980s hit TV show *The A-Team*, and through his famous one-liners and elaborate dress sense has become a legend of popular culture. Within this site, expect to find the most outrageous references to the plane-fearing action man in the form of replica dolls, toys and artwork. My personal favourite is Mr T in-car satellite-navigation system, where you are personally directed by the man himself, but be warned: he doesn't like it when you take a wrong turn – fool!

http://www.mrtandme.com

★ ★

HEALTH AND MEDICINE

WITH SO MUCH information obtainable to us on the Internet, it's no wonder we can virtually become our own doctors. Reading up on illnesses, diseases and cures is common practice and the amount of knowledge gained from web sources is as good as infinite. However, we must be careful where we receive our information from, since not all websites are backed by reputable medical sources, as you will see in this chapter. But, on the whole, the Internet has opened up a window to a wealth of health and medical information that many will have been kept in the dark about. With technology moving so fast now, the world of medicine is brought straight into our homes, where it can be referred to at the click of a mouse, which I'm sure most people find very reassuring.

:: RECOVERING EMOTIONS

Suffering from a trauma? Forgotten how to feel? Eric will help you recover that loss. You simply request the emotion you are no longer sure you relate to and Eric will act it out for you. There's a catalogue of more than two hundred emotional experiences to choose from, including simple ones such as happy and sad to the more complicated such as breaking wind subtly in a supermarket-checkout queue, being caught downloading pornography at work and discovering a hamster in your underpants. Eric is currently working on new material that includes feeling Swedish, and realising your life-size Elvis doll has been stolen.

http://www.emotioneric.com

★ ★

:: QUESTIONABLE MEDICAL DEVICES

This site is where the curator of the Museum of Questionable Medical Devices shares his collection of the hilarious, horrifying and preposterous medical devices that have been foisted upon the public in their quest for good health over the ages. It includes the Prostate Gland Warmer, Phrenology Machine, Recto Rotor, Nose Straightener, Wonder Electro Marvel and hundreds of other quack devices to cure your ailments. And, if this website isn't enough for you, visit the museum itself in Minnesota, USA, for an up-close and personal viewing, putting all speculation to rest.

http://www.mtn.org/quack

★ ★

:: ABORTION TV

Before you enter this site, I must warn you there are images that may be disturbing to some people. The site's intention is to shock its viewers on a subject that they feel has not been addressed properly in schools, by governments and in abortion clinics. Through the use of videos, pictures and news on the topic of abortion, they aim to arm people with all the facts before they make a life-changing decision. An educational site with an open, honest approach, if a little hard-hitting at times, which aims to turn around the way people think and feel about a procedure that holds many dark and disturbing secrets.

http://www.abortiontv.com

★ ★

:: WAITING ROOM

A sensitive and informative site for those unfortunate people having to live with the tragic fact that a loved one, after suffering a terrible trauma, is in hospital in a coma. You may find yourself alone and troubled and beginning a frustrating period of waiting that could go on for months with no change. This website aims to help you get through this terrible time by providing you with an online support group in the form of a virtual waiting room. On entering the room, you will be met by the website's author, attorney Gordon S Johnson, who will talk you through the content of the website. He has had 15 years of experience in representing and supporting the victims and families of brain injury, and continues to do so through the means of this website.

http://www.waiting.com

★ ★

:: EMBARRASSING PROBLEMS

Have you got a problem that you feel you can't share with a friend for fear they won't understand? Visit the site of Dr Margaret Stearn, a professional in the field of advising people like you on your most embarrassing problems. With her sympathetic yet direct approach, she will endeavour to put right whatever is wrong by listening to what you have to say and professionally and privately giving you advice. This is your one-stop health-education shop for all your wellbeing- and body-related issues. So, if you are suffering from anal bleeding, or maybe you have a bout of the old restless legs, our girl is here to help in the best way she knows how.

http://www.embarrassingproblems.co.uk

★ ★

:: COMPUTER MEDICINE

Everybody suffers from one day to the next with computer problems. Either your computer is running too slow, or it crashes for no reason, or maybe files that you have been saving have just disappeared. But have you ever thought that maybe computers have bad days just as we humans do, and sometimes don't perform as well as they should? The scientists at the Institute of Holistic Computer Wellness have found that ideas from holistic medicine have actually improved some computers' performance and have vastly reduced intermittent computer failures. There are many remedies and techniques that can be found on this site such as the Natural Food Filter, whereby hooking up a lemon to your PC will increase the computer's organic electricity, making it a more natural process. Visit this site for more astounding theories on the topic of homeopathy for your PC.

http://users.bestweb.net/~bennetc/holistic

★ ★

:: REAL AGE

Are you constantly being told you don't look your age? Maybe you are blessed with youthful skin and an athletic body and are often told you look much younger than you really are. Well, the people at Real Age are here to shock you into reality by asking you a multitude of questions about every aspect of your lifestyle, ranging from what you put in your mouth to whether or not you wear a seat belt in the car. After you have completed the questionnaire, they will determine what your real age is in response to your answers. You will probably be shocked to find that you're not as young as you thought. But fear not: the team at Real Age will knock you up a plan that will give you all the information you need, getting you back down to the youthful age you once were.

http://www.realage.com/index.aspx

★ ★

:: MILK SUCKS

Have you ever thought about how drinking milk affects you, your body and the rest of the world? My guess is probably not, and until viewing this site I was quite ignorant to most facts about milk other than the fact that it comes from cows. This website is an anti-milk site, protesting, educating and informing its visitors on all facts surrounding milk. From birth, most of us are brought up on the white stuff and are taught that it provides a good source of calcium that will make us grow up big and strong. That may be so, but there is always another side to a story and the creators of Milk Sucks wish to tell you theirs.

http://www.milksucks.com

★ ★

:: NIGHT TERRORS

Do you find it hard to sleep at night for fear that you'll have a bad dream? Or maybe you find yourself waking suddenly from a nightmare. Night Terrors is a website created by someone who suffers just like you and wants to help support you in combating these sleepless nights. Visit this site for a breakdown of different sleep disorders and why they come about, or read through stories of night terrors, sent in by site viewers, to expand your knowledge surrounding sleep disorders. Or you could just take my advice of no cheese or chocolate before bed, and definitely no *Nightmare on Elm Street* viewing.

http://www.nightterrors.org

★ ★

:: MIND CONTROL

This website holds a collection of interesting links to pages and sites that depict drug testing and government mind control throughout history. Find out about the CIA's relationship with LSD in the 1950s, or read through the painful diaries of victims of electronic mind control. A disturbing, eye-opening site that holds many an alarming secret, which some may find amusing while others will be horrified.

http://www.gpc.edu/~shale/humanities/composition/assignments/experiment/lsd.html

★ ★

:: MIRACLES OF MODERN MEDICINE

What would you say if I told you that you could genetically modify the profile of your unborn child and achieve male pregnancy? You would probably think I was having you on, but this is the website of RYT Hospital, run by Dr Liu, and its affiliate, Dwayne University Medical College, which carry out more clinical trials utilising the latest technological advances than anywhere else in the world. Visit the page of artist Lee Mingwei, who the RYT claim is the first male to get pregnant, and read through his astonishing story to parenthood. Another interesting place to visit on this site is Clyven, the world's first transgenic mouse with human intelligence. Groundbreaking stuff here, guys.

http://www.rythospital.com

★ ★

:: DESIGNER VAGINA

Ladies, are you suffering from stress due to the lack of love you have for your lady garden? Are you not reaching your sexual potential due to wear and tear of your overused front bottom? Are you fed up with the fact that your once pruned bush now resembles a pair of beef curtains? Well, let Robert A Jason put you right again. Dr Jason is the founder and medical director of the Laser Vaginal Rejuvenation Institute and aims to meet the patient's individual physical and sexual needs through surgical enhancements to the vagina. Don't waste hours of time on your pelvic-floor exercises. With one of many different procedures to choose from, Dr Jason and his team will have you popping out ping-pongs in no time at all.

http://www.lvri-ny.com

★ ★

:: FAECAL DEODORISER

A common problem in households around the world is that of smelly toilets. Anyone who has had the unfortunate experience of using the bathroom directly after someone who has just dropped the kids off at the pool will be elated to discover this website. Whiff is a new revolutionary poop deodoriser pill that literally eliminates the smell of bowel waste before it leaves your body. The pill, which is to be taken orally, contains only natural ingredients used safely for centuries by Chinese and Native American herbalists. It nourishes and promotes the presence of 'friendly' bifidobacteria and lactobacilli in the digestive system, leaving you with almost odourless poop. Going to the toilet after a curry will never be the same again.

http://www.takeawhiff.com

★ ★

:: WORLDWIDE WOUNDS

This website is your online guide to treating every kind of flesh wound imaginable and should come in handy for any potential injuries you may get or are currently suffering from but can't seem to heal. It's a bible for mothers with young children, but it's not for the faint-hearted or those with a queasy disposition. Find out the best way to care for your wound in the form of dressings and treatments, or for a more natural approach try looking at the maggot-therapy section!

http://www.worldwidewounds.com

★ ★

:: THE PHOBIA LIST

Do you find yourself being scared of almost everything? Or maybe you just have a strange infatuation with pressing people's buttons. Well, the Phobia List is here to dissect all of your phobia queries by cataloguing them alphabetically for your viewing pleasure. Read up on phobia facts and where their names originated; or, if it's help with a phobia that you're after, check out some of the links. I'd just like to take this opportunity to say to anyone suffering from either cyberphobia or bibliophobia that I am greatly sorry for any discomfort I may have caused you, but well done for getting this far – your pain is now over!

http://phobialist.com

★ ★